PORTFOLIO POWER

▶ The New Way to Showcase All
Your Job Skills and Experiences

PORTFOLIO POWER

▶ The New Way to Showcase All
Your Job Skills and Experiences

MARTIN KIMELDORF
WITH A FOREWORD BY JOYCE LAIN KENNEDY

Peterson's

Princeton, New Jersey

Other books by Martin Kimeldorf:
Educator's Job Search
Creating Portfolios For Success in School, Work, and Life
Serious Play, A Guidebook to Leisure Wellness

Visit Peterson's Education Center on the Internet (World Wide Web) at http://www.petersons.com

Library of Congress Cataloging-in-Publication Data

Kimeldorf, Martin.
    Portfolio Power : the new way to showcase all your job skills and experience / by Martin Kimeldorf : with a foreword by Joyce Lain Kennedy.

    p.   cm.
    Includes index.
    ISBN 1-56079-761-4
    1. Applications for positions.   2. Job hunting.   3. Career changes.
I. Title.
HF5383.K4815   1997
650.14—DC21   97-3499
                                                                          CIP

Editorial direction by Carol Hupping   Composition by Gary Rozmierski
Production supervision by Bernadette Boylan   Creative direction by Linda Huber
Copyediting by Kathleen Salazar   Interior design by Cynthia Boone

Printed in the United States of America
10 9 8 7 6 5 4 3 2

CONTENTS

Foreword   vii
Acknowledgments   ix
Introduction   1

PART I   YOUR PORTFOLIO OF TALENTS   9

Chapter 1   The Power of Professional Portfolios   11
Showcasing Your Skills and Accomplishments

Chapter 2   Developing a Portfolio Mind-Set   17
Creating Your Own Personal Portfolio First

Chapter 3   Career Portfolios   31
Getting Started on Assembling Your Career Portfolio

Chapter 4   The Job Search Portfolio   59
Using a Portfolio in Job Hunting, Interviewing, and Self-Marketing

Chapter 5   The Career Advancement Portfolio   73
Using a Portfolio in Performance Reviews and for Raises and Promotions

Chapter 6   The Lifelong Learning Portfolio   79
Managing Your Learning Assets to Stay Competitive

Chapter 7   From Khaki to Civvies   87
Documenting Military Skills and Accomplishments for Civilian
Employment Opportunities

PART II   PERFORMING PORTFOLIO ALCHEMY   97

Chapter 8   Just the Artifacts   99
Creative Approaches to Collecting and Crafting Artifacts

Chapter 9   Content and Captions   105
Selecting the Contents and Writing Supporting Text

Chapter 10   Organization   113
Methods for Grouping and Sequencing: Chronological, Functional,
Thematic, Specialized

Chapter 11   Adding the Designer's Touch   125
General Design Principles and Construction Tips; Developing
Your Front Matter and Closing

Chapter 12   The Final Review   141
Evaluating Your Completed Portfolio

Chapter 13   The Virtual Portfolio   147
Creating and Using an Electronic Portfolio

Conclusion   165

Appendix A   Suggestions for Personal Portfolios   167
Appendix B   Suggestions for Professional Portfolios   169
Appendix C   Skill Words   173
Appendix D   Personality Words   177

Resources   179

Index   185

FOREWORD

You won't find a book like this anywhere. Go ahead—look! The shelves of bookstore business sections are littered with books on every aspect of the job search—every aspect but one: portfolios. Many professionals in the field are unfamiliar with their powers, and this unfamiliarity is reflected in the extreme lack of resources on creating a portfolio. This obscurity can't last much longer because the portfolio is among the strongest of career tools, facilitating everything from self-evaluation to promotions to job changes.

The timing for this work is perfect. In today's harsh job market, a strong portfolio can help secure you a very cozy place, but you had better do it right. Luckily, by reading this groundbreaking book, you've come to the portfolio guru: Martin Kimeldorf. He is the only authoritative published source on the subject.

It's getting meaner and faster out there every day: Economies worldwide are restructuring and laying off "nonessential" employees. As professional competitors, we all have to get a little tougher. You may find that the portfolio is a force to safeguard you from unexpected downsizing.

Why?

Because it can be an in-depth demonstration of your indispensability and employability in today's volatile environment. Not only do we have to get tougher, we also have to keep up the pace. As we near the turn of the century, computer technology has overtaken all other discoveries. A portfolio may translate your employment candidacy not only on the spot and in living color but also on-line for recruiters—a portfolio allows you to deliver a cyberspace image of yourself as one who is utterly up-to-speed.

Do It Right

Despite all its power potential, without the right tools, your portfolio may merely display disaster. *Portfolio Power* helps you prepare for and create a portfolio that means business. In showing you how to psyche yourself up and collect data, Martin Kimeldorf pioneers the mechanics of holistic, personal, and professional portfolio preparation, with as much vim and vigor as the best of career books. I'm truly delighted to see this work on the shelves. It answers questions I'm hearing more and more frequently:

> *What is a portfolio? Do you need help to make a portfolio? What can you do with a compilation of your own personal or professional successes? How do you begin to create a portfolio? Can a stack of papers really get*

you that promotion? How can you be sure that your portfolio meets your employer's standards? What belongs in a portfolio? What should you leave out? What will really sell you? What kind of image gets you the jobs you've always wanted? How would you like to hit your next position's priorities on target with projects you have already done? How would you like to get your foot in the door marked "employment" before the interview?

Who uses portfolios? In years past, portfolios were mainly the province of artists and designers, models and writers. Now, portfolios are surfacing in a number of fields, ranging from education to business. Individuals have adopted the portfolio as a way to graphically demonstrate they have plenty of talent to sell.

A Valuable Guide

Martin Kimeldorf shows you how to present your power packages with more than the sparse pages of generalizations and objectives that define the typical résumé. He shows you the ropes of conjuring up your best skills in tangible form—in charts, graphs, letters, and work samples.

You can confidently create masterful portfolios by following his advice as he shows you how to:

- Develop a collection of data for the portfolio's content

- Analyze that data critically, prioritizing each portfolio element to target different employers

- Plot your career goals or changes using the portfolio

- Target your portfolio toward your own line of work

- Check your final product for details

Martin Kimeldorf does not stop at illustrating the mechanics of how to create a portfolio: He shows you how to keep your career smiling in today's ever-changing work environment. This book is about preparedness, competitiveness, and negotiating for better jobs. It's about selling you at your best, at your top value. In his easy-to-use process, Kimeldorf leads you through stages of professional evaluation and analysis of previous employment. He helps you define skills toward a more focused, employable individual. Far more than just an exercise in portfolio building, Martin Kimeldorf's guidance can lead you to places you've always wanted to go but never knew how to reach.

Joyce Lain Kennedy
Syndicated Careers Columnist

ACKNOWLEDGMENTS

Many people offered their assistance as this book evolved. Their many helping hands and heads were invaluable in the development of *Portfolio Power*.

My Gifted Editor
I want to thank Carol Hupping for being in my corner on this project.

The Trusted Advisers
The following people shared portfolio stories and advice. Their anecdotes helped document the emerging use of portfolios in colleges, business, foreign countries, and the labor market at large. Their patience and support contributed greatly to my work:
Anna Miller-Tiedeman, Bill Vick, Carol Harberger, Catherine Smith, Dave Beam, Donald Pitre, Gail Dunham, Gary Morrison, Harry Drier, Howard Kimeldorf, Jack Chapman, Jane Sanborn, John Pignato, Joe Stimac, Judith Leng, Ken Schlueter, Leni Donlan, Margaret F. Riley, Marty Thornton, Nancy Sheely, Patrik Muzila, Phil Shapiro, Sue Sherbert, Thom Rakes

Reliable Readers
I am indebted to the following people who generously offered invaluable editorial feedback on the manuscript in its different stages:
Pam Mortillaro, Sara Yada, Gail Dunham, and Marlene Tebben

Community Inspirers
I'd like to thank the gang at the Four Seasons Book Store in Olympia, Washington, who first planted the seed for this book in my overwrought brain.

(**Note:** When first and last names are used in the text, they come from real-life stories. When only a first name is used, the anecdote represents an amalgam of various experiences, and any resemblance to actual persons living or dead is coincidental.)

INTRODUCTION

Today, a good education, strong credentials, loyalty, and hard work are no longer automatically rewarded with a promotion or the promise of job security. It is doubtful that most of us will even find the promised land of lifetime, perpetual employment. We are entering an era where fewer promises are kept between employer and employee. This means we've got to become self-reliant, to take responsibility for our own careers—think like a job coach and act like our own employment agency. We have to learn or acquire new skills as old ones become obsolete or less competitive, and we need to maintain a record of our achievements and learn how to effectively market our talents to potential employers or clients.

I can't guarantee that a portfolio will get you a job or that every employer will want to see your portfolio. But I can say with confidence that collecting samples and crafting a portfolio showcasing your accomplishments will increase your power to communicate your worth to employers, customers, or clients. Over twenty years ago, I discovered that portfolio power was not limited to artists or financial planners. I found the portfolio to be the perfect tool for both chronicling a career and telling my lifework story.

My Portfolio Credentials

I came to the professional portfolio concept in a rather circuitous manner. The story of this process illustrates how a portfolio can weave the various strands of one's lifework experience into a compelling story that will convince others of your potential worth.

After earning my degree in liberal arts, I was ready to spread my wings and leave my sleepy college town in the Pacific Northwest for the bright lights of New York City. After arriving, I tried different day jobs ranging from bank teller to machinist. This allowed me to spend the rest of my time gorging on the Big Apple's cultural life. I continued my personal studies of playwriting, art, and technology. And, because my uncle and aunt were well-connected to the creative souls dwelling in Greenwich Village, I had many opportunities to see how artists lived their lives, along with the chance to see the works of many gifted people, some of which were displayed in portfolios.

Three years later I was enticed with a scholarship to return to Oregon and enroll in an industrial-education teaching program. I relished the career-change opportunity.

In preparation for seeking employment as a teacher, I knew I wanted to convey both sides of my background: liberal arts and technology education. I wanted to work for a school that would appreciate my interdisciplinary bent, my deep desire to integrate the aesthetic eye with the skilled hands of a craftsperson, and in the mid-1970s I chose to communicate this with my first professional portfolio. It contained a summary of all my college classes, letters of references, and notes of appreciation from parents and colleagues. In addition, I included poetry written by my at-risk students, photos of products I had created in the university's technology labs, an essay I wrote about careers and the changing nature of work and technology, a list of my play productions, and articles from newspapers featuring the alternative education program I coordinated for the campus YMCA/YWCA.

I was one of the first in my graduating class to get a teaching contract. By the end of the 1970s, I returned to college to earn a master's degree in special education, adding more pages to my portfolio.

I've never had a problem securing an offer during an interview. I attribute a large part of that success to my portfolio presentations, because they allow me the opportunity to go beyond the routine interview questions. I believe that the artifacts in my portfolio speak volumes about the kind of employee I know I can be. I have also used samples from my portfolio to secure offers for writing books on job finding, leisure, and community service.

Over the years, I found that a portfolio could assist me in both my personal growth and professional explorations. In the late 1970s I crafted my first personal portfolio containing sketches, plans, and technique sheets supporting my studies of wood carving. More recently, in 1993–94, I assembled a portfolio for my first painting exhibit. Portfolios have become valuable companions on my journey, serving me well in the hunt for work, pursuit of play, and the search for meaningfulness.

A Hiring Experience

Let me illustrate the power of a portfolio with a recent hiring experience of mine. One of our support staff members quit a few days prior to the start-up of a new cycle of work, and I had approximately 48 hours to hire a replacement. I did the usual preparations, networking with people about any available qualified individuals and developing a list of interview questions designed to probe the candidates in increasing depth. While the time line was less than ideal, it is a far more typical situation than you might imagine.

I was amazed to see who showed up. In these desperate times, I found myself interviewing people with many more qualifications than those listed in the job description. One person had taught college, another served as an administrator, and still others had years of experience. Selecting the single best candidate became a vexing task. I knew from past experience I did not want to limit my choice to the individual offering the best answers to the interview questions because, too often, this results in choosing the person who is best with words as opposed to the one who would perform best on the job.

Like a thirsty man searching for water, I scanned for any additional clues. As a result, anyone who brought something besides "words" to the interview table received my undivided attention. Two candidates showed up with collections of reference letters. Ah, here were additional, external opinions I could add to my own intuitive examination of the candidates.

Now imagine how I would have reacted if someone had brought in a portfolio. Suppose I could leaf through a binder containing an employee evaluation sheet with high marks for "flexibility" and "thoroughness." The next page might contain a letter from the United Way applauding fund-raising efforts that exceeded the established goal, which would serve as a testimonial to the interviewee's initiative. A certificate from a workshop on mentoring would tell me that the job seeker possesses people skills and an interest in coaching or serving others. A printout from a database designed by the candidate illustrates technical skills. As I question further, I learn that the individual is a self-taught programmer, demonstrating the capacity to solve problems as a self-directed learner. What more could I ask?

Why Now?

In the late 1980s, educators in the United States as well as in other countries rediscovered portfolios and began to utilize them in instruction and student evaluations. Early experiments were done in the humanities, where students archived various papers, projects, and samples in their school portfolios. By the mid-1990s, the portfolio became an accepted tool within the larger framework of educational reform. Students were asked to critically evaluate their work and then proceed to revise their best pieces for a final grade. It was hoped that students would look more closely at the quality of their efforts, perhaps adopting the posture of an artist or writer who takes his or her work seriously. I wrote my first book on the subject—a student portfolio workbook—in the early 1990s.

In 1995 a fortuitous event signaled me it was time to write a portfolio book for adults. It began as a weekend presentation and book signing in my local bookstore. I approached the event with many doubts: Who did I really think would come to a student workbook presentation on a beautiful and sunny Pacific Northwest Saturday morning? To my astonishment, I was greeted by a full house of eager, bright-eyed faces! Only about half the group were teachers, and I was equally surprised to find that the attendees represented a wide range of ages, from 20-something to late midlife. They had not come to learn about student portfolios but rather to ask questions about their own professional portfolios and their uses.

Two months after the bookstore event, Marty Thornton (who directs adult education in two school districts in Maine) sent a letter confirming my intuitions. She had given a workshop to a large and enthusiastic audience at a women's business conference on developing professional portfolios. "I think there is a big need to explore this topic for adults," she wrote.

Next, I contacted various experts working in either the career field or school-portfolio movement. Judith Arter, an expert at the Northwest Regional Education Lab, wrote back, "I think people develop portfolios for themselves all the time even though they may not call it that. Scrapbooks, albums, and memory boxes are all forms of portfolios; a purposeful collection of artifacts."

Jane Sanborn, who does similar work in a San Francisco education lab, suggested that the renewed interest in portfolios may reflect people's heightened sense of insecurity and the subsequent feeling that one should take nothing for granted, including the longevity of one's job. To stay at the ready for an emergency job search, many people may feel a need to "document their growth and progress" for use in next year's, next month's, or even next week's job search.

Catherine Smith, who promotes employment portfolios in Michigan's department of education, wrote me, "I think there is tremendous need, especially as people face downsizing, restructuring, and career change, to find a way to document our strengths. This is particularly important when you realize that many employers are discouraged from writing letters of reference these days due to litigation and other issues."

Portfolio Stories

Today there are many more portfolio stories to tell. Let me share with you some of the portfolio stories I have collected based on reports from people across the country and around the world. You will see that portfolios are being used not just to get jobs but also during employee reviews and as a tool for managing lifelong learning and skill upgrading.

For instance, executives in one East Coast county government are using portfolios to select and guide the development of a new generation of leaders and managers. One person, who landed a new job that moved him up from an assistant director to a director, told me that his portfolio preceded his arrival on the new job and helped pave the way: "My portfolio was passed around for almost a month after I got there. They could see in-depth what my emphasis had been recently and the skills and focus I would probably bring to the position. I do feel it really helped establish my credibility with the rest of the staff in the office."

In an e-mail to me, a Canadian man described his successful career in a $2-billion Canadian automotive retail chain where he was the director of human resources. This was followed by work as an executive-level manager and a consultant. During my on-line interviews with him, he told me that he used portfolios as part of his overall job-search and marketing strategy. He wrote, "[The portfolios] improved my reach and netted me more clients, phone call follow-ups, and interviews than relying on a résumé alone."

In the Menomonie, Wisconsin, school district, both new and experienced teachers must now submit portfolios when applying for positions. To ensure that these portfolios meet its needs, the district has set up guidelines to simplify the process of constructing a portfolio. It must include samples or evidence of work in six areas, including communicating with families, lifelong learning, teamwork, community involvement, and professional performance. The people involved in the hiring are confident that portfolios have improved their selection process.

Catherine Smith has talked with many employers in Michigan about portfolios and has summed up her thoughts in her aptly titled book in progress *Make Your Case*. She urges people to think of the communication process as a trial in which one must present evidence of one's potential and encourages her readers to think of their professional portfolios as "Exhibit A." If you can prove your capabilities or demonstrate your talents in a convincing manner, you will find more open doors in today's labor market, schools, and business circles.

Creating Portfolios is Easier Than You Think

A portfolio shares many qualities with the products and projects with which you are already familiar. If you've ever kept a journal, archived artifacts in a scrapbook, or cataloged your vacation in a photo album, then portfolios will be a natural for you. In fact, once they're created, they are easier to maintain than the traditional text-based résumé.

My first portfolio grew out of my journal writing habits. In the quietude of a diary, I recorded my observations and thoughts, explored my daydreams, and asked the big questions. I filled pages with notes or quotes from books I was reading. Gradually, I expanded my purpose and added sketches, plan sheets for future projects, and photographs. Using dabs of paste, I glued in postcards, itineraries, brochures, maps, employee evaluations, certificates, awards, and newspaper clippings. The journal transformed itself into an ongoing scrapbook.

Sometimes, in the midst of a stressful period, I find solace and comfort in going back over my old scrapbooks and journals because they remind me that challenges today are no more insurmountable than those in the past. When I want to create a professional portfolio, I select and organize specific items to showcase talents for employers, customers, or others who might be interested in investing in the promise I possess. Later, I might put away the portfolio binder and go back to writing in my journal or pasting photos into my scrapbooks. Life is a back-and-forth process alternating between work and play, personal and professional passions.

I guarantee that after you assemble a portfolio, your world will seem less fragmented because you will discover a larger connectedness running through your lifework. You'll gain an enhanced sense of purpose and satisfaction as you gaze upon your collected artifacts, knowing more completely who you are and what you're about.

What This Book Will Do For You

In the pages that follow, you will learn a great deal more than you now know about what portfolios are and how they can be used. Lists, exercises, and step-by-step directions will help you assemble your own professional portfolio that can be used, in variations, for most all of your career needs. You'll be challenged to think deeply about your life and then creatively sum up your interests and abilities. As a result, you'll be able to more effectively market your "assets" and remain on the front edge of a labor market increasingly defined by competition and uncertainty.

Part I of this book is designed to give you an overview of the professional and personal portfolios and their uses. Chapter 1 sets the tone for the entire book by defining the portfolio and its power to enhance your career. Chapter 2 introduces you to the *portfolio mind-set*. You'll be introduced to the informal personal portfolio, which is a great way to begin building the habit of collecting and organizing content. If you're comfortable with the portfolio concept, you may want to dive right into chapter 3, which includes activities and lists to help you begin designing a general-purpose career portfolio. This leads right into chapter 4, which illustrates how to prepare and use your professional portfolio in a job search, during job interviews, and in marketing yourself as a freelancer or contractor. Chapter 5 tops off the process with suggestions for using a portfolio to advance on the job. Later chapters cover special-purpose portfolios such as those used in making the transition from military to civilian work.

Part II gets down to the nitty-gritty of crafting your portfolio. You'll be taken step by step through the process of selecting artifacts in chapter 8 and writing captions in chapter 9. You'll learn how to design an aesthetically pleasing package and review methods for effective presentations in chapters 10 and 11. At the end of the process, in chapter 12, you'll find out how to evaluate your portfolio to be sure that it is a balanced and a complete reflection of you and all your assets. And finally, in chapter 13, you'll explore the possibilities of creating electronic portfolios using simple, everyday computer software, as well as advanced multimedia programs, and distributing these portfolios on the World Wide Web on the Internet.

I have tried to design this book for maximum flexibility, because everyone will come to it with a different need. You can skip around and just read or complete those activities that mean the most to you. As you read, ask yourself, "Does this new approach really fit my style? Does it match the realities of my unique situation, career, or occupation?"

Keep in mind that there is no set portfolio format. Portfolios come in many shapes and sizes. Since there is no single correct way to make a portfolio, consider this book only as a starting point, upon which you can base your own portfolio experiments.

Once you achieve a more complete sense of what you have to offer, you will be more effective at competing for work opportunities. As a result, you can more confidently make decisions about career changes; write better résumés; offer more details on loan forms or scholarship or job applications; answer interview questions more convincingly; and network more effectively for advice and information. The portfolio, ultimately, is your story, shaped by your pursuit of a fulfilling career.

Let me close by inviting you to step forward and examine the portfolio of talents you have inherited and those that you've worked so hard to develop over the years. Hopefully this book will enable you to use your aptitudes wisely in your quest for challenge, recognition, and satisfaction.

PART I

Your Portfolio of Talents

In the very human race for opportunity, the competition seems to escalate with each passing decade. We compete in this lifelong career marathon for prizes in school, the labor market, and the business world. In the past many people had the same job for several years; some even retired from the company they started with, after thirty years of service. But, as we know, the nature of employment has changed a great deal.

Historically, artists, writers, and designers have used portfolios to market their talents as they searched for temporary projects or freelance work. Today, more and more of us find that our work lives resemble those of the artists, who move from job to job. As at least one career counselor has said: "The only permanent truth about work today is that most of it is temporary." The time is right for all job seekers to use a portfolio. It's the perfect vehicle for showcasing talents and experiences. It can succinctly tell your story and prove your potential.

1

THE POWER OF PROFESSIONAL PORTFOLIOS

Showcasing Your Skills and Accomplishments

▶ The professional portfolio: Think of it as a collection in progress, a place where you store those things related to your training, work experience, contributions, and special accomplishments. It is the place to document all your work-related talents and accomplishments so that you have a good sense of your "assets." As you gain a clear understanding of your lifework story, you'll increase your ability to see your potential and communicate it to others. This newly gained insight can assist you in assessing where you are on your career track.

Such a portfolio can serve you in a host of career tasks. You can go back to this collection each time you begin a new job search, seek advancement, or change career direction and take from it those items that will be most useful.

On the job, you will find it useful to document your contributions for future performance evaluations. This type of portfolio could include samples of how you increased profits, developed new systems approaches, solved problems, completed specialized training programs, adapted new procedures, and so forth. When you find yourself in the middle of a performance interview and you're asked to demonstrate a skill, your portfolio will make a stunning visual aid. When it comes time for the annual review of your work, you might find your employer focusing less on your job title and duties and more on your projects and outcomes. A portfolio containing evidence of contributions at work (log of work hours, awards, thank-you notes, special project descriptions) may help secure the promotion or raise you seek.

If you decide to look for new work, you can take pieces from this portfolio to create a job search portfolio, which, along with your résumé, helps you market your talents to prospective employers.

What's in a Portfolio?

The first syllable of the word *portfolio* comes from a Latin root *port*, meaning *to move*. The second syllable, *folio*, means *papers or artifacts*. So a portfolio is a portable collection of papers and/or artifacts.

Most all professional portfolios contain letters of reference, résumés, lists of accomplishments, and samples of work. Now, as such portfolios become more important as job search tools, they can include much more: artifacts and samples that showcase one's communication skills (memos, reports, conference evaluations), people skills (agendas from committees, customer ratings, summary of training workshops), and technical skills (samples from manuals, job evaluations, photos of finished products, lists of services delivered).

Should you move on to start your own business, you can pull samples and artifacts from your professional portfolio to create a business portfolio that becomes a self-marketing tool for selling services to clients. You can take your portfolio to the bank and include it in your business plan proposal or use it to help gain financial support: a loan from a bank, a government grant, investment partners.

If you go back to school for more training or an advanced degree in preparation for your next job or career change, you can add to or adapt your professional portfolio for use in a request for scholarships and grants. You can use it to document your learning or assist you in your transition from school to work. A portfolio cross-referenced to a college curriculum could assist you in earning credit for prior work and learning experiences.

A Portfolio for the Competitive Edge

Artists, designers, photographers, and advertising account executives have been using portfolios for years to showcase their talents. In financial circles, people work with investment portfolios. Salespeople often show customers a portfolio of their products or services. Pilots and captains document their efforts in flight and ship logs. Writers often present a portfolio of their work to editors and publishers. Actors and models share photographs with their clients. Sometimes the record goes beyond the written page as when engineers bring drawings as well as models to a presentation, a television director shows up with a videotape, and an Internet artist, or webmaster, brings a disk to an interview.

In today's tough job market, there's more competition than ever for jobs and promotions, and if you want that job or promotion, you've got to prove yourself during the interview or performance evaluation. Everyone is looking for a way to increase their power to articulate their talents and accomplishments. It's time to expand beyond the spoken word and bland résumé by adding the punch of a portfolio presentation.

The Employer-Friendly Job Search Portfolio

Perhaps the most compelling reason for creating a professional portfolio lies in the employer-friendly nature of the document. While it is not a magic bullet, it does possess the power to transform the murky exchange of business communication into a focused conversation, supported by concrete examples. One outstanding work sample is worth a thousand résumé words.

In yesterday's labor market, career counselors were quick to point out the ineptitude of most job seekers. Some books cited the fact that only 1 in 200 job seekers ever had a decent job-search education. As a result, most people used outmoded job-seeking skills (e.g., relying on want ads) and went to interviews totally unprepared to describe or sell their abilities. Ever since the mid-70s, when layoffs and downsizing became a fact of life in the work world, most Americans have become far more savvy. Many more job seekers today know about networking and enter interviews with answers they've already prepared for the "top twenty tough questions."

As job seekers improve their job-hunting skills, it's not so easy to pick out the best one anymore. What's an employer to do when so many candidates claim they are the greatest thing since sliced bread, that they each have what it takes: energy and drive, teamwork, communication skills, analytical qualities, entrepreneurial sense?

How can an employer know what is real in a world full of hype and hyperbole? One envisions a stressed-out manager, worn to the nubs by the eighth interview, rising from the chair and desperately demanding, as did Sergeant Joe Friday in the old TV show *Dragnet*: "Words, words, words! Give me just the facts, ma'am [or sir], just the facts!"

This is where you enter with your portfolio. At the interview, you can present the facts, or more accurately, the artifacts.

THE PROFESSIONAL PORTFOLIO AS A METAPHOR FOR OUR TIMES

Businesses, agencies, and schools are being called upon to perform many more functions than ever before. As a result, today's employers are likely to solve a work problem by hiring temporary workers with special talents rather than constantly training and retraining a permanent staff. Consequently, your very employment—indeed, even your competitive edge—is built on continually upgrading or expanding your skills in a lifelong learning process. Developing a portfolio of varied skills is a strategic way to create "employment insurance." Used in this sense, the word *portfolio* becomes a metaphor that represents a shift in thinking, away from job titles and toward the skills and learning you acquire as you move from job to job or from school to work—and back again.

Professional vs. Personal Portfolios

The professional portfolio is designed to showcase your talents as you compete with others for a new job, a raise, a promotion. If you're self-employed, your portfolio can be used to demonstrate your talents to new clients and customers. By contrast, a personal portfolio is a collection that you keep for yourself—scrapbooks, photo albums, family trees, personal journals.

Though the audience is different, you may find that your professional and personal portfolios overlap. A membership card from a computer club or a picture showing you demonstrating software at a local computer users group meeting speaks eloquently to your ability to master complex software, train others, and keep up with the latest technology in your profession. Your travel itineraries and grades from foreign language courses could be used in a professional portfolio to demonstrate your foreign language skills when interviewing for a position as a workplace diversity manager in a human resources department or perhaps for an inner-city counseling role.

DON'T PUT OFF TILL TOMORROW . . .

Dismiss the notion that you'll get around to making a portfolio the next time you go job hunting. Learn from Carol Harberger why it is far easier to begin one now rather than waiting until the day you get called for an interview.

Carol recently went looking for a job as a school administrator. She found an opening in the spring and was invited to an interview. When she called to confirm a time for the interview, the secretary said that candidates could bring a portfolio. Unsure of how to go about making a professional portfolio, Carol went searching for information on the Internet. She found some material I had uploaded, and she e-mailed me the following message:

> I searched for information about professional portfolios without much success until I found your book for students in the on-line library. Your material gave me some ideas and reminded me to relax and enjoy the process. Having a portfolio wasn't mandatory for the interview—and yet I feel it's a good opportunity to stop and reflect more widely. Most important, I feel it's crucial that we demonstrate the same skills of portfolio-making that we ask of our students.
>
> I really didn't have a model to use so I tried to organize the "pieces" I'd assembled, not knowing how their significance would translate to strangers without being accompanied by explanatory notes. I also wanted it to be changeable so I could later add or delete materials.
>
> I used a white binder with clear slip-in cover, showing my name and the words: "WHO I AM." The various sections of my portfolio were

divided with the same buff-color paper I used on my cover, and I used a graceful font throughout to give my work a unified look. There was also a short introduction. Each section page simply began with an action word or phrase similar to the heading one might find on a résumé. I used words and phrases like collaborating, growing and learning, and envisioning. After each section page, there were several exhibits illustrating related skills. For example, my artifacts supporting communication skills included faculty bulletins and memos, handbooks I had written, and quotations I collect to inspire people. In another section, I tried to convey how I mix work with play by using education-related cartoons, a humorous children's bookmark, business cards, and a computer disk. I ended my portfolio with a huge card given to me by my students.

You may not need to rush out and create a portfolio right now, but you should begin the collection and reflection processes. At this point, you're at the thinking stage that precedes construction. A later chapter will guide you through the process of creating a final, polished professional portfolio.

First Steps in Creating Your Professional Portfolio

Are you feeling uneasy because you've never assembled a portfolio? Let me reassure you, it's really quite easy. You probably have most of the artifacts you need already. Don't purchase a binder and plastic sheet covers right this second. At this point, the best preparation is to use the following exercise to stimulate your thinking about what you might want to put in a portfolio or, for the time being, in a shoe box or manila folder.

Review the exercise first and determine if you are ready to start building your professional portfolio. You may want to go on to the next chapter and begin with the simpler, more informal task of creating a personal portfolio. Alternately, if Exercise #1 gets you enthused, then move ahead to chapter 4 and begin planning how to use your portfolio for job seeking and interviewing.

▶ EXERCISE #1
Professional Portfolio Warm-Up Exercise

This activity is designed to get you thinking about what you might collect for a professional portfolio. Turn to Appendix A: Suggestions for Professional Portfolios—and look at the items listed there; they'll give you ideas about what you might want to collect.

In this exercise you'll look at typical items from work (work samples) that could be included in your professional portfolio.

EXERCISE #1 Continued

1. Review Appendix A. See if you can come up with a list of ten to twenty items you can lay your hands on that speak to your employability. Look at items you might have at school, home, and work. Don't forget your study, attic, boxes in the garage, and desk at home for items related not just to your current job but past employment as well. Write down as many items as you can think of now, then put the list down and come back to it a few times over the next several days; you'll get better results if you spread out this part of the exercise over a few days.

2. After each item, jot down a skill or two you associate with that item.

3. Then rate each skill's importance for your current job. Rate it as though you were hiring your replacement. Then separate the list into *Skills Used Today* and *Skills to Use in the Future*. Put these lists aside for future reference so you can revisit and add to them as you go through this book.

Now that you've been introduced to what a professional portfolio can do for you and how you can begin to create one, let's begin by exploring personal portfolios in the next chapter. This will serve as an excellent entrée into what I call the portfolio mind-set.

2

DEVELOPING A PORTFOLIO MIND-SET

Creating Your Own Personal Portfolio First

▶ Putting together a personal portfolio is a great way to get into the portfolio mind-set. Once you've gone through the process of creating a personal collection—or even just reading about doing it in this chapter—the task of collecting and archiving samples becomes effortless and, dare I say, fun. The personal portfolio necessitates a conversation with yourself and evolves into discourse about who you are. This becomes an excellent jumping-off point for a later dialogue in which you'll describe yourself to others through a professional portfolio.

THE CONTINUUM OF LIFEWORK DOCUMENTS: JOURNALS TO PORTFOLIOS

In my home office, journals, project binders, and portfolios soldier up along the bookshelves, each representing a different time in my life. They stand ready to serve my needs when I want to reminisce, supply samples for a grant proposal, or assemble a portfolio for an interview.

And although each volume is bound in some fashion, the partitioning of life into separate booklets is only an illusion. The attempt to place documents from one's life into neatly bound portfolios reflects our human desire for a sense of order rather than a presumed orderliness in life. The covers are only convenient boundary lines.

This can be more aptly illustrated by examining how three candidates—an artist, a teacher, and a grandparent—used their lifework documents.

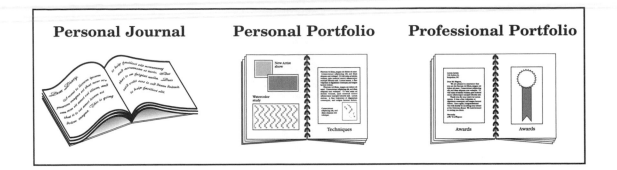

Personal Journal   **Personal Portfolio**   **Professional Portfolio**

Laura began with an interest in sketching and filled five journal volumes with images from her outdoor studies. Occasionally she would add entries about new techniques she heard about or read about in art magazines. As her interest grew, she decided to try some formal training at the local college. It was just what she needed—she gained direction, stimulation, ideas, and inspiration from others who shared her interests in color, shape, line, and space. Soon, watercolor became her favorite medium, and she began adding color photos of her favorite watercolorists' works to her journal. At first she imitated the paintings of those she most admired. Then ever so gradually, a style of her own emerged.

When her teacher recommended Laura's work be included in the all-school exhibit, Laura submitted a portfolio of her favorite pieces and a short essay describing what she was trying to accomplish. What began as a personal sketching journal transformed itself into a personal portfolio where her style took root. When the time was ripe, it was easy to compile a professional portfolio for the judges. Looking back over her early sketching journals, she was able to identify the enduring themes and techniques that formed the basis of her style.

Geo came to the United States from the Philippines in the 1980s—he'd been a teacher in his homeland and hoped to someday be one in his adopted country. After he arrived, he set up a binder to keep track of important vocabulary words and phrases. It grew into a scrapbook when he added pictures and copies of practical documents (rental agreements, advertisements, loan forms, driver's license information, bus routes). Within three months, he signed up as a volunteer English teacher at the local refugee center and began using his binder as a teaching tool. Geo was very good at what he did, and he continued to build his portfolio, adding to it lesson plans, thank-you notes from his students, and ultimately an entire curriculum.

During Career Day at the local university, he showed the binder to a counselor, who quickly recommended the teacher education program for Geo. His slim personal project binder grew into a voluminous portfolio documenting his teaching ability: lesson plans, articles about the refuge center language program, certificates for volunteer work, letters and pictures from grateful students, a copy of the scholarship award of merit, and his teaching evaluations.

Jana retired last February from a high-powered management job in the Department of Corrections. As a department leader, she was accustomed to a schedule full of committee meetings, public speaking, and report writing. At retirement, she woke up to an empty calendar—which left her wondering, "Who am I, really?" After two months of trying to keep herself busy, she settled on the task of conducting a personal review of her life. Jana gathered up the baby books she wrote as a young mother, the family photo albums, and her professional portfolio, which included articles, awards, and résumés. She embarked on creating a memoir for her children and grandchildren.

The experience satisfied Jana's deeply felt need to make sense of her life, to sum it up, to think about where it would go next. She took the final product to a journal writing class and found herself expanding upon the project, filling many, many pages.

One day Jana wandered back to where she used to work. She wasn't sure why, but she started at the human resource department and stopped in to see an old friend, Lily. Jana described what she had been doing with journals and memoirs. Lily was intrigued for two reasons—first, she was thinking about retirement herself, and, second, she was trying to make a traditional retirement planning seminar (that stressed financial planning) more meaningful for the employees. They met later for drinks, and as Lily took a look at Jana's personal portfolio, an idea surfaced. "Why not come and present a seminar about the process you went through?" Lily asked Jana. "Maybe this should be done as part of our retirement workshop."

Later that night, Jana wrote in her journal, "I don't know why I went back to the department today; maybe I was hungry for validation from someone at work." Two years later Jana had published her memoir as a workbook for retirement planning. Her schedule is again full as she cruises along in her second career—leading retirement workshops.

Mutual Support Through Building Personal and Professional Portfolios

Laura, Geo, and Jana all began their portfolios out of a natural desire to collect their thoughts about art, English, accomplishments, and life experiences, among other things. For all three, the initial collection grew and took on a larger purpose: the search for fulfillment. The process illustrates how a hobby or personal quest often leads to the development of a skill or knowledge that has value later in one's career.

One never knows how the collected artifacts will finally be used or organized. Whether for personal or professional use, the portfolio often serves a subconscious or subtle purpose, and the very act of collecting and cataloging the items bestows a degree of organization in one's life.

The more formal the organization and presentation, the larger the potential audience for that product. Geo ended up sharing his binder with total strangers at a career day. Jana's more personal and informal portfolio (baby books) is primarily for showing to a smaller audience of family and friends, while Laura's presentation at an all-school exhibit requires a more formally designed portfolio.

Often, people travel back and forth between personal and professional goals, personal and professional portfolios. At any moment, Laura, Geo, or Jana might return to their diaries or personal portfolios. Laura might tire of her painting style and choose to explore other artists or return to free-form sketching in her journal. Her next personal portfolio might center on the study of oil painting. Geo could start a new binder about a third language. Jana may want to begin a portfolio about her life as a grandmother.

Personal Portfolios Help Integrate Our Experiences

Most of us will probably need to accept the fact that the work we perform tomorrow will probably be different from the work we do today. Therefore, as our career journey continues, we need to assess our entire range of skills and experiences, regardless where we acquired them. The flexible nature of portfolios makes them the perfect vehicle for keeping track of our kaleidoscopic lives.

The portfolio is primarily a collection, and when you get into the portfolio mind-set, you can see your personal life and career as a collection of talents rather than defining your life by a single job title or a single role. People who possess portfolio mind-sets are better able to evaluate the totality of their experiences and skills. This integrated outlook reflects today's lifestyles. We define our lives by the variety of roles we play: an employee during the day, a mother of two in the evenings and weekends, an individual in our leisure time who enjoys gardening, golfing, bicycling, or whatever. We view ourselves as multifaceted beings. We're all wearing many hats, trading in the old chapeaux for new ones, watching our hair go gray, and wondering what outfit we'll wear next. The portfolio forces us to look across this spectrum of experience and integrate these fragmentary "pieces of our existence."

THE PERSONAL PORTFOLIO—A NATURAL BEGINNING

It's really quite easy to begin a personal portfolio. You can take what you already know about the commonplace scrapbook or photo album and turn it into something very creative and engaging. It can take on many different forms, matching the mood or stage you are in. One woman I know made a collection of thank-you notes that she reviewed on blue days. A music lover might choose to archive sheet music, recorded music, or posters of shows. Wordsmiths take pleasure in story quotes, scraps of poetry, and sayings. A person who enjoys working with tools or the outdoors includes handtool catalogs, seed packages, pictures of restored antique cars, and blueprints for wooden furniture. Travelers bring back hotel brochures, printed itineraries, bills from hotels, postcards, and menus.

The Memory Book—A Special-Purpose Portfolio

A personal portfolio can serve a very special purpose. It can be constructed around a single event signifying a rite of passage such as a birth, retirement, graduation, or wedding.

In the early 1990s, I created a memory book for my widowed aunt in New York City. Her husband had first come to Manhattan in the 1930s with dreams of writing an opera. After they were married in the 1950s, they spent the next forty-plus years actively involved in the cultural diversity of Greenwich Village. When my Uncle AT (Alex Tamkin) passed away, it was very difficult on my Aunt Sloan. She tried to keep track of things by writing little notes, but everything piled up until she couldn't see the ceiling. When Sloan decided it was finally time to leave her beloved city, I created a very personal portfolio that would assist her in recalling our shared experiences, and I called it a memory book.

▶ EXERCISE #2
Personal Portfolio Warm-Up Exercise

Developing the portfolio mind-set requires that you slightly alter how you look at the world. Posters, conference flyers, icons, labels, receipts, postcards, memos . . . all the physical things in your world begin to take on an additional dimension. Everyday objects come into sharper focus as we consider which of them we want to cast in our portfolio script. To acquire this sensitivity, one must slow down a bit; finger things more thoughtfully; pause, nod, and tuck a thought away (a healthy thing to do in a hurried-up world, whether you're creating a portfolio or not!).

Take a moment now to assess what you already have collected in your life. Everyone treasures some things, be it baseball caps, dolls, recipes, art, or wind-up toys. What objects just seem to casually collect on our bookshelves and mantles or in the hidden-away drawers? By thinking about them, you'll become more conscious of the power of artifacts and more aware of the value in collecting items.

In this exercise, consider objects people typically collect and then come up with your own list. Look at Appendix A: Suggestions for Personal Portfolios. Fill your mind with possibilities, explore where you live and where you work, look at your world with a different view. Remember, a starter list is just that, a beginning point.

1. Make a list of ten things you generally collect, actively or casually. You won't be able to write all ten in one sitting, so you can add to the list over time. Appendix B gives you the ideas you need.

2. Ask yourself this question: What kind of person do these objects describe? Think of the artifacts as clues in a mystery. Imagine that someone moved into your house and

EXERCISE #2 Continued

discovered these items. He or she tries to guess what kind of person you are. How might this person describe you? Make three smaller lists describing the style of working, learning style, and skills or aptitudes demonstrated in your longer list of ten items. What might a collection of postcards placed on a world map reveal about you? A detective might surmise that you inspire loyalty, enjoy using organizational skills, and perhaps speak more than one language. A tool bench cluttered with wood carving tools, sketches, and notes speaks about a person who is comfortable with ambiguity, possessing good eye-hand coordination or mechanical aptitude, and possibly is a self-directed learner.

3. Pick out two or more items you might consider including in a portfolio about your life. Don't be surprised if this exercise suggests ideas that could relate to a professional portfolio.

WARMING UP TO ARTIFACTS

The next two exercises will help you build beginning portfolio skills as you translate the portfolio mind-set into portfolio-making activities. These two exercises are adapted from another work of mine *Authoring Your Days* that covers journal-keeping. I've chosen these journal-writing exercises as starting points because creating a personal journal is the first step toward creating a personal and then a professional portfolio.

These exercises are designed to help you heighten your awareness of the artifacts that already exist in your life and examine what these items reveal about you.

▶ # EXERCISE #3
Examining Seasonal Artifacts

Each season brings its own cycle of work and leaves in its wake various markers of what has transpired. The clues about ourselves that we leave behind on the trail might include check stubs for a Thanksgiving holiday, bills for outdoor gardening, a Christmas card list, or simply old to-do lists and appointment calendars. It seems that each month or each season, we're involved in some kind of bookkeeping task. These are familiar "artifacts."

Locate some common artifacts that could serve as clues about how you spent your time last year. It can be anything you regularly collect and could include things like checkbooks, business ledgers, matchbook covers, old ticket stubs, receipts, old envelopes or stamps, postcards, birthday cards, photos, or whatever you tend to collect (or forget to throw out). These items are really miniature time capsules containing the relics of our lives. Like looking at a snapshot, it will be easy to go back in time and recall things from the past using these items as prompts. My wife, for instance, keeps her calendars for years. Each summer she looks over how the year went and reflects on what has transpired.

On a piece of paper or in a journal, make a list of things you have collected on a regular basis that contain information about your past year. Let this list germinate in your mind. Then pick a private time to study or review the artifacts you have been able to round up. Recall the stories behind certain checks, matchbooks, ticket stubs, receipts, etc. Don't write just yet; linger a bit more in the moments you are recalling.

Then ask the pivotal questions: "What do these items suggest about my life? What do these clues-of-living tell about my accomplishments, problems, pace of life, priorities, skills or talents, worries, thoughts, or feelings? What people are included in this evidence? What themes run through my life?" Think of yourself as a private eye or anthropologist, looking upon the artifacts as clues about the times in which you live. Write your thoughts in a journal.

▶ EXERCISE #4
The Party Game

Each employer wants to know what skills you can bring to the job or project. This involves an evaluation of one's past experiences, interests, and talents. It is important to examine not just the talents you have shown at school or work today but also the ones you have used in your community, family, and leisure experiences. You may also need to consider the skills you hope to acquire in the future.

To help you see the possibilities, project yourself into a future celebration of a rite of passage. In this exercise, you visualize an important turning point in your future life. It might be graduation, retirement, a wedding. This critical stage is marked by a party honoring your passage into a new phase of life. You'll visualize the party and the artifacts that are on display tables commemorating your efforts; you'll "hear" the voices and speeches describing your life.

(Note: This activity is designed to appeal to many different thinking or learning styles, and it is, therefore, longer than most exercises. In order to sustain this role-playing or visualizing effort, you may find it helpful to complete this activity across several days rather than all at once.)

1. Imagine where the party will take place. Would it be in a home, a restaurant, or a community center? The place will be decorated with your favorite color and filled with your favorite sounds. Close your eyes for a moment, and try to paint a mental

EXERCISE #4 Continued

picture of what it would look like. You may want to then draw a floor plan showing the decorations, chairs, tables, and general layout of the room. Finish the sketch by writing the lyrics or title to your favorite music near a picture of the sound system.

2. Suddenly, the music is turned down, and the lights come up. This person hosting the party says:

> *Ladies and gentlemen, please take a seat. It's time to begin the toast. As you know, several people couldn't be here tonight, but they did take the time to send in a tape. They wanted to send a personal message about our guest of honor. We liked the idea so much that we asked several of the guest of honor's closest friends, teachers, and family members to add to the tape. They all wanted you to know how our special guest fit into their lives.*

Think about people you might have helped in your life and those who have helped or influenced you. This could be someone who needed your advice in making a decision or someone you helped through a tough personal or school experience. Think about people who asked you to show them how to do something. Consider people who took the time to teach or show *you* something. List the people who would be proud to say they were associated with you at some point in their lives. In a journal, record who might be there and what they might say about you as they introduce their tape. Let this sit for a day or so before going on.

3. Use the previous testimonials to help identify your people skills. Go back and circle phrases or words that indicate a talent or ability in the previous step.

4. The slide show is next. It contains pictures of the different ways you have used your hands creatively, whether it involves manual or creative labors, chores, or technical wizardry. Draw six squares to represent six slides in this show. In each box, list or describe what could be contained. Consider any tool, machine, equipment, or special material you enjoy using. Review what is in the garage, sewing room, kitchen, yard, rehearsal room, at work, at camp or hunting sites, at the gym, and in the game room, loft or den. Let this sit for a day or so before going on.

5. What kind of skills or abilities does the slide show indicate? List three or more physical skills or talents.

6. Finally, it's time to turn your sights on your intellectual pursuits. This is demonstrated on a display table that people examine just before sitting down to the main meal. This table contains samples of your work, showing facts and figures, words and ideas.

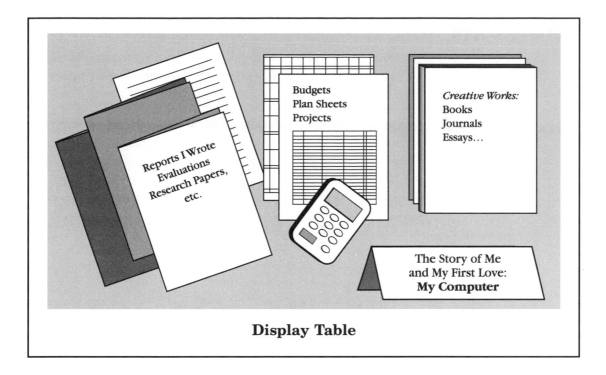

Display Table

Here are some things that could go on a display table of this sort:

- Birthday and anniversary cards you made for people

- Your favorite books or magazines

- Items you used in calculations (spreadsheets, calculators, math books)

- Samples of personal or expressive writing (letters, journals, stories, poetry, music, memoirs)

- Samples of professional writing (grants, proposals, presentations, brochures, reports, newsletters, guidelines)

- Examples of ways you stay organized (calendars, organizer, items you collect or archive, portfolios, albums)

- Visual displays (charts, graphs, tables)

What would be found on your table? Draw it and label the items.

7. It's been a great night! You feel very honored that these people shared this time with you—it has been very meaningful. After looking over your life, you may realize that you never really thought about all of the talents you had. Maybe you have always thought of yourself as average. But now you recognize that you have many special

EXERCISE #4 Continued

talents that have meant something to you as well as others. Now for the grand finale: The host starts up the music, people take their seats, and we hear the following words:

Folks, I would like to end with a special awards ceremony. You know, too often we go through life without knowing how much we mattered. Unfortunately, many of us never receive an award, and that's too bad. Tonight we're going to change that for our special guest. We have asked a few people who have worked with our honored guest to come forward and present a special award. We have three plaques to give out tonight. They describe the special personal qualities, talents, and contributions of our guest of honor!

In your journal, brainstorm about the possible awards you might receive. Don't limit yourself to just three awards—generate as many ideas as you can. To help in this process, review everything you've thought about up to this point in this exercise: the testimonials, the slide show, the table display. You could get additional ideas by looking over the skills listed in Appendix C: Skill Words or the traits enumerated in Appendix D: Personality Words.

8. Let your list sit for a day or two and then pare it down to three possible awards. These awards should represent what you are proudest of, what you would like to be remembered for, and qualities or skills you would enjoy helping others acquire. On your next to last journal page, make a drawing of these three awards.

9. On the very last journal page, review and reflect upon this entire exercise. Consider the following questions:

- How do you feel about this party?

- Were you surprised at all the talents listed?

- Will anything you listed change in the future?

- What artifacts are suggested for your personal portfolio?

DEVELOPING THE ARCHIVING HABIT

Journal writing is a circular feeding process: The writer fills the journal, then the journal fills the writer. The same can be said for keepers of portfolios. Reviewing a portfolio of work achievements fills the soul with the promise of tomorrow, journeys waiting to be taken. It all begins with the simple and ultimately profound act of collecting.

For me, archiving was a natural. I come from a family of born archivists. My father was a scientist and tinker. His workbench was framed by row upon row of jars and plastic boxes filled with bolts, fasteners, electrical connectors, rubber and plastic gizmos, and things that still remain a mystery to me. He collected all kinds of tools, including miniature clock repair kits, portable hand-held routers, and other special-purpose paraphernalia. His library was full of photos, odd X rays from his lab, and specimens from tide pools. And there were the albums, scrapbooks, and file cabinets containing precious thoughts expressed in essays, articles, recipes, cartoons, and quotes from famous people. My mother was the "administrative coordinator" and her domain extended to organizing bills, various chores, playing the piano, dancing, and entertaining us with bubbly conversation. She had the incredible task of orchestrating the chaotic tendencies of her three feisty sons and their daydreaming father.

I follow in my parents' footsteps. It's not hard. I began keeping scrapbooks and journals during high school. The tendency to archive, write journals, and construct portfolios was encoded on my chromosomes, and this has kept me in touch with some of the best parts of my living. Furthermore, the value of my "stuff" seems to grow every year, at a rate far exceeding the index of leading economic indicators.

I would guess that storing, collecting, and documenting is far more common in your life than you might imagine. Think about all the things you already collect: receipts for the IRS, records of conversations with your boss about projects, photos of your home furnishings that are locked in a safe-deposit box for insurance purposes. Some of us who work in the public eye must keep detailed records of the services we render to others, correspondence, and even phone logs. People in the military often keep scrapbooks to chronicle their tours of duty; in fact, commercial products have been designed to hold photos, patches, awards, and other odd-sized military artifacts. (See Resources near the back of the book for one source for these.) Documentation and storage is now a way of life, and some businesses make a living from it.

I believe that most of us already possess an archiving ethic or attitude. Archiving for a portfolio builds upon our general tendency to store and collect, and that's why you'll find it inherently easy and natural.

Portfolios are built around your archiving habit. The simplest approach is to consider everything of even passing interest to be of value. Put it all in a big file folder or box and consider it your "working portfolio" that can then serve either your personal or professional needs. Then, after six to twelve months, sift through the collection and remove things that no longer seem as important as they once did. Sort what remains into piles of related items. You determine the criteria. You could start with just two piles, personal and professional.

After your piles grow too large for their containers, break each pile down into piles based on general themes such as leisure, community, family, job, accomplishments, leadership samples, job search techniques. Eventually, the

Humoring Ourselves

Self-absorption can become like thick glue in the archiving process. The inner search can become so self-satisfying that we get stuck at this stage of portfolio building. If you find this happening to you, do what I do: use humor to "unstick" yourself. In the balmy flicker of a laugh, you can gain breathing room and time to achieve some balance between the serious and comic elements of your life.

Stop and conjure up funny sayings, look for humorous imagery, poke fun at the whole affair—jest for the heck of it! Ask yourself, "What humorous applications might my portfolio serve?" Four starter ideas are listed below.

- When trying to get parental approval to date someone, use the portfolio to prove you are not a member of an antisocial group.

- If you get tired of being asked at parties, "What do you do?" take out your bulging three-ring binder with large letters inscribed on the cover: *My Fifty-Year Portfolio.* Offer to sit and review the entire contents over the next several hours.

- When the writers for your favorite sitcom go dry, offer to mail them your portfolio as a source for new ideas that spring from the divine human comedy.

- When guests stay too long after dinner, offer to show them your portfolio.

names of each pile will suggest labels for boxes or larger envelopes. Then as you store things, you can quickly sort them and put them in their proper place. The labels also make it easier to find things later. When you can quickly store and retrieve items, you know that you've acquired the archiving habit.

Cataloging Artifacts

A collection becomes an archive when the contents are organized and ultimately easy to retrieve. As your archive grows, you'll find it helpful to keep a list of the contents somewhere. I prefer doing this on my computer because I can search for things electronically much faster than by hand.

In addition to listing each artifact on a master list, add a few facts about each item. This is known as *cataloging artifacts*. It pays off later when you must hastily assemble a portfolio because the catalog descriptions can be quickly turned into captions or summaries. Cataloging each item as you toss it into your working portfolio takes only a moment and saves hours later. I learned this lesson when I began keeping a list of the conferences at which I had made presentations. A few years later I went to review my compilation of public-speaking experiences and realized that forgetting to consistently record the date and title of each presentation made the information practically useless.

Take time to catalog artifacts in detail. This is doubly important for any artifact that might eventually be transferred to a professional portfolio. In general, try to record the who, when, what, where, and why represented by the artifact. Some questions you might consider addressing in your catalog notes about particulars surrounding an artifact include:

- Who was there?

- When did it take place?

- Where was it? What happened?

- Why was it important? What did it represent?

- What challenge did I have to overcome?

- What were the benefits or outcomes of the effort?

- What skills do I think this artifact could represent?

In case you need to check on things later, be sure to include any important contact information such as the names of people, phone numbers, addresses. This information will be important for both your résumé and portfolio. Store it in a computer file or attach your notes to the artifact itself for future reference.

3

CAREER PORTFOLIOS

Getting Started on Assembling Your Career Portfolio

▶ The career portfolio is one of the richest and most powerful ways to portray your lifework story. Because it contains samples from all the different kinds of work you do—paid, volunteer, education, home—it effectively chronicles your career journey. This portfolio will comprise the most comprehensive picture available of you and your work capabilities. The contents of your career portfolio will help you in three distinct ways. It will:

1. Assess your career direction (i.e., choosing a first career, getting a good sense of where you are on your present career track, helping you decide on a career change)

2. Provide information and documents that will be useful in future job searches

3. Document your on-the-job accomplishments for use during job performance evaluations and discussions of raises and promotions

In addition, the contents of your career portfolio can also be used for marketing your services or products in freelance or self-employment work, as well as linking your learning to your overall career development.

The items you collect for these purposes often overlap and can be kept together in a working or general career portfolio. If you change directions in your work, a review of the artifacts in your career portfolio can help renew your confidence in your potential and may suggest new talent combinations that could steer you toward new occupations. A positive employee evaluation that you've saved can be used later in a job-search portfolio that you take to interviews. Work samples testifying to your contributions to committees, overtime efforts, or mentoring coworkers can be used in a performance-evaluation portfolio when you go for your annual review or when you seek a raise or promotion.

While later chapters will specifically address creating and using smaller and more targeted portfolios for job hunting and interviewing, performance evaluations, and self-marketing, this chapter explores how to use a portfolio for documenting all your work experiences and skill development.

If you are already clear about your career direction or if you are in the midst of a job search campaign, then you may want to move ahead to the later section, "Taking Your Portfolio on Informational Interviews," in this chapter or move right on to chapter 4.

HOW YOUR PORTFOLIO FITS INTO TODAY'S AND TOMORROW'S BIG WORK PICTURE

Before going further into career portfolios, it may be helpful to pause and consider the larger trends sculpting the present and future patterns of work. Only by understanding the bigger picture can we truly appreciate how a portfolio fits into the ever-changing labor market of today and tomorrow.

As the twentieth century draws to a close, many authorities in the field of labor and economics predict that the way work will be distributed and performed will bear little resemblance to the system of jobs and occupations known to the last five generations. According to these experts of labor and economics, the number of people with full-time permanent jobs will dwindle in the next century, and part-time work and temporary assignments could become far more common than in the past.

Current trends support this prediction. William Bridges notes in his book *Jobshift* that the employer with the largest payroll on any given day is not IBM or General Motors but temporary work agencies such as Manpower, Inc. A recent study by Michigan State University found that four out of ten college graduates were accepting employment in temporary or time-limited contract positions. An October 1, 1995, *Seattle Times* article contained the startling observation that if all the temporary employees worked under one roof, they would constitute Washington State's largest employer.

Whether you are permanent or temporary, the majority of the people will probably draw income from a variety of sources such as paid work, home business, contract or temporary jobs, and consulting. Business book author Charles Handy (*The Age of Unreason*) describes this variegated income stream as a "portfolio of work." Neil Peterson, who supplies temporary executives through Execu-Temps, observes that "companies look to individual portfolios" that demonstrate what a person can bring to the job. In the current wave of short-term work, employers want flexible managers who can use their talents on a variety of projects.

As permanence disappears from job descriptions, we enter a piecemeal work world where the tempo of one's assignments seems more random than routine. It may become commonplace to collect fees for services rather than rely only on a single source of income or a permanent paycheck. As this trend grows, people will come to view all of their skills as either marketable or tradable. For instance, I might work part-time as a teacher and sell my tutoring services at night. When I want to vacation at my accountant's lake cabin, I'll offer to do groundskeeping chores in exchange for a week's rent. I could write an advertising brochure as payment to the fellow who cleans my roof.

Jeremy Rifkin describes how the workplace will continue to shrink and relocate in his book *The End of Work, the Decline of the Global Labor Force and the Dawn of the Post-Market Era*. Rifkin agrees with Handy and Bridges that we have entered a new era where mass permanent labor will be increasingly replaced by work done with small groups of elite workers, augmented by intelligent technologies and a contingency workforce. He envisions a future of automated or workerless factories that become "virtual companies." In his scenario, a virtual manufacturer outsources or subcontracts everything from manufacturing a product to marketing, delivery, and repair. The virtual manufacturer becomes a broker of services, a conceptualizer of ideas, occupying a slimmed-down office space, directing a small staff, and constantly contracting the temporary labor of others.

Regardless of which role you play in the future work scenario, one thing is certain—people will live and work longer and, as a result, change jobs more often than any previous generation. As noted earlier, this is bound to change the way employers and job seekers look at work. And, because the way we work is changing, we must also change the way we search for work. The only constant you can be sure of is that your job will probably not be there forever. In a larger sense, we are all becoming "temporary" workers and full-time work-opportunity seekers.

The brave new world of work is evolving toward a state of constant motion, where workers are continually moving on to various projects, teams, or companies. In the most basic of terms, it means you are no longer your job title, but, rather, a collection of talents or skills moving from one site to another. The portfolio becomes the perfect tool for highlighting these portable skills.

THINK OF YOUR CAREER PORTFOLIO AS A CATALOG OF YOUR SKILLS

The career-portfolio format reflects the shift from job titles and departmental fiefdoms toward organizations using project-oriented teams and cross-functional workers assembled around various temporary assignments. In this new scheme, organizations flatten the hierarchy, remove layers of middle management, and come to depend on self-directed teams pursuing outcomes rather than turfdoms. A career portfolio matches this new way of working and has the advantage of demonstrating your talents across a broad range of assignments, departments, and teams. Your catalog of work samples speaks to outcomes rather than the inanimate facts and job titles listed on an application or résumé.

By adopting the portfolio mind-set discussed in chapter 2, you'll lay the groundwork for participating in the labor market of tomorrow. In the process, you will be compelled to rethink your work identity. In the true spirit of the word *career*, your lifework will return to its linguistic root that means *course*. Looking over the course of your career journey, you'll want to capture the essential themes, passions, and abilities that define your life and that have value for others.

To get a good sense of what a career portfolio is, think of it as a variation on a financial portfolio. Your investments in your career portfolio are represented not by dollars but by months spent on projects—hours in classes earning advanced degrees, updating skills, getting your recertification—and by years on the job. Each unit of time reflects either experience or training that can be invested and reinvested over and over in different companies. Managing your career portfolio means you need to regularly diversify and reorganize your investments. In other words, you'll need to continually reexamine your assets and recombine them to fit new, and as yet unknown, opportunities. To maximize your worth, you will probably need to invest in lifelong learning opportunities and document the additional knowledge and skills gained in these learning experiences. (See chapter 6 for a detailed discussion of lifelong learning portfolios.)

People looking for work must examine the totality of their skills. Since you never know how you'll earn your daily bread next, don't limit your perception of your future employability to the skills you used on your last few jobs.

Career experts encourage people to think of themselves in terms of skill sets or cross-functional skills. Once you factor out all the skills you possess, you can then consider how these skills might be transferred to other places and other kinds of work. Skill-factoring exercises will follow shortly in this chapter, but for now, consider this example:

Suppose you are an unemployed teacher who's looking for job postings on an electronic bulletin board or in the newspaper. Your best bet is to avoid limiting your search to key words such as *teacher* or *educator*. Rather, break down your job into its many components and look for words or synonyms that suggest extensions of your skills into new areas. For instance, as a teacher, you might investigate work as a trainer, curriculum developer, or technical writer. Upon further reflection, you also realize that teaching involves the ability to organize, negotiate, use humor in the workplace, and communicate effectively. In this fashion, you really begin to move away from job titles and refocus your attention on your entire set of skills. As you change your outlook or mind-set, new occupations and even different industries come into view.

GET INTO THE ARCHIVING HABIT

In the ideal scenario, you collect artifacts as you go, storing them in a working career portfolio. Later you cull from the entire collection the samples that best match a unique project or job you'd like to be hired for or promoted into. From these you manufacture a portfolio product tailored to a specific opportunity.

In reality, the process of maintaining a career portfolio is less linear and more often follows a reciprocating pattern. Sometimes you look at an artifact first and then consider the skills it represents. Other times, especially while trying to connect with a position or promotion, you focus exclusively on a work opportunity and then scramble to collect (or create) work samples that best match the employer's needs.

Once having begun the process of developing a working career portfolio, you simply add to it as you go. At any time you can repackage the "story" to fit the work opportunity you are seeking. This hands-on product easily and quickly adapts to your career needs. And because it is not dependent on words and your writing ability alone, most people will find it easier to construct than a résumé.

When archiving as you go, it is always best to collect with the broadest goal possible rather than narrowing your focus to your current job. If you only archive items from work, you may miss an opportunity to collect a valuable expression of your talents outside of the workplace. And since the average person uses only about half of his or her talents in paid work, you would be cutting yourself off from valuable artifacts. When you are unsure whether or not to keep an item, place it in a personal portfolio if you are keeping one (see chapter 2); later you can move it into your career portfolio if you discover that it's an asset to your work life.

The following exercises are designed to help you with the first stage in career development and decision making. These activities can help you assess your talents and interests. As you consider your work values and aptitudes, review your work history, and take an inventory of your skills, you begin to formulate a clearer picture of who you are and where you want to go. This vision helps answer the question "What should I be collecting?"

CRAFTING THE CAREER PORTFOLIO

Career-portfolio production begins with a self-examination of your entire lifework experience. The act of assembling the facts and evidence can help you answer the big question so many of us ask ourselves: "What do I want to do next in my career?"

This method works best when you forget your limits, releasing the shackles of doubt, and concentrate on "what could be." Begin by asking yourself, "What is my source of happiness?" Make an inventory of those experiences, studies, tasks, hobbies, tasks, projects, and random moments that have brought joy, satisfaction, and a sense of accomplishment or real meaning into your life. As you think about these events, try to analyze or identify the skills and talents being used.

Suppose you have fond memories of the praise you received for the colorful brochure you designed for a neighborhood emergency team program. Next, consider other times you expressed yourself with visual elements such as company memos or report covers, designing a display or project training board. Finally, determine what you might call these related experiences. This general name will then become the descriptor for a general skill that you can transfer from work site to work site. Once you understand how your skills can transfer from one type of work to another, you'll find it less difficult to envision the options. A portfolio filled with examples of your transferable skills prompts you to think about your possible career alternatives.

THINK ABOUT YOUR SKILLS IN BROAD TERMS

Suppose your hospital has just finished another round of planning for budget reductions, and, shortly, you'll become an unemployed nurse. Perhaps you are thinking about leaving the field anyway, but every time you list your experiences, it seems to spell out one job title: "nurse." You feel constrained by the fact that most of your experience or training has been in nursing. To get beyond this constraint, you'll need to look past the narrow technical things you do and consider the much larger set of skills used throughout your working life. This is called *skill-factoring*, and it involves analyzing your old job duties and experiences from a different perspective.

For example, handling patients requires the use of sophisticated people skills. Let's face it—individuals who don't feel well often are in pain and may not display their best side. Your ability to comfort these people, to ignore their aggressive or angry outbursts, suggests that you might possess a talent that can be transferred to other people-intensive environments such as emergency response work, counseling and referral, or customer relations. You begin by asking, "What is it I do to put people at ease?" Do you share your personal interests in an environment that seems impersonal and bureaucratic? Do you show concern for your patients' emotional well-being when others don't? Are you able to maintain a stable profile because you don't depend on your job for everything; you have other sources of happiness?

One nurse used her interest in wellness to start a skin-care and self-care store. She also specialized in support products such as wigs for women undergoing cancer treatment. Another nurse left her hospital to provide AIDS-prevention training in a county outreach program. And another enrolled in additional computer courses that prepared her to work as a consultant on a new information system used to automate recordkeeping that was formerly done by her staff.

These examples illustrate what happens when a person begins to relate a general skill of "working with difficult people" and applies it to specific work tasks in other settings. In this way, the career changer analyzes the "cross-functional" nature of the general skills and then groups and regroups the skills into different "skill sets." Each skill set applies to a specific occupational slot.

Consider the following skill sets and sample artifacts of a nurse. You can use the sample process, even the same categories, to start with—then change the technical items and examples to reflect your own occupational area.

Lifelong Learning or Advanced Studies
- Continuing education certificates or pretests/posttests
- Training aids or products developed for patients or nurses
- Summary listing of trends and techniques studied related to the field

Communication or Persuasion Abilities
- Annual evaluations from peers or managers highlighting communication or charting skills
- Thank-you notes from patient mentioning my empathy or listening skills
- Written documents: reports, pamphlet, brochures, flyers, proposals for in-service
- Tape of oral presentations at conferences, seminars, or staff meetings

Managerial or Leadership Skills
- Memos that inform or persuade
- Picture of group I am leading
- Summary of changes I proposed or designed: delivery of care services, reassignments during job restructure, representing nurses to other departments
- Samples from planning training, in-service, or conferences
- Committee work in which I developed protocols, care plans, clinical pathways, or procedures

Information-Gathering Talents
- Researching medical problems on the World Wide Web
- Gathering results from reference searches in the professional medical library
- Sample designs for a survey instrument about patient satisfaction
- Written summary of laws and policies affecting the service delivery

The following exercises are designed to help you analyze your own database of talents in terms that extend far beyond your recent or current job title. If you have trouble getting started, you might want to go back to chapter 2 and complete a personal portfolio. You may also want to complete an in-depth self-assessment like those you'll find in many good career books, such as *What Color Is Your Parachute?* by Richard Bolles or *I Could Do Anything If I Only Knew What It Was* by Barbara Sher.

▶ # EXERCISE #5
Compiling a Lifework Database for Your Portfolio

The process of career assessment begins with the compilation of a lifework database. This is nothing more than a review or summary of your work and training experiences. The word *work* must be taken in a general sense and should include any and all forms of work, no matter what shape that work takes or how it is rewarded.

Begin by listing all of your significant work experiences. Include experiences in paid jobs, volunteer work, internships, and apprenticeships. Review any part-time or temporary work, freelance or contract work, home-based business, and any other form of self-employment. In addition, include the times you were asked to share your expertise even without being paid, like the time you helped your neighbor set up her ham radio station. If you have limited experience, then factor in any formal education or self-study experiences, and don't neglect hobbies or community service. Examine anything you really enjoy doing and are good at. You'll experience a liberating feeling when you define the words *skill* and *work* in this manner.

I like to put data about my past experiences in columns or charts because it helps me to visually summarize many different thoughts in a small space. As I look down, across, and diagonally at information in the chart, I discover new relationships and new possibilities. I view the chart as a puzzle with squares full of clues. (If you wish, cut out the squares by hand or on your computer, and rearrange them to find new combinations.)

Begin by filling in the column on the left of your chart. List the times and places related to your work and training. In this column, list your last job or learning experience. Leave

Lifework Database

Time, Places, and Position	Major Duties or Responsibilities
1992–1996 LMN Inc. Community Representative and Training Coordinator	Promoted positive image in community Hosted monthly recruiting meetings Reviewed environmental impact statements Kept records and made monthly reports Designed staff training
1988–1992 Evergreen College Student	Majored in business management and training

some blank spots every now and then, because you'll probably remember something later. Then repeat the process down this column, until you cover information from the last ten to fifteen years or until you review several time periods in your life. When you are finished with the left-hand column, compile a listing of the major duties, responsibilities, work, or tasks you performed for each item listed.

Here is a sample of a chart partially completed. Please note that many more items could have been listed under *Major Duties or Responsibilities*.

While this may seem similar to completing a job application, here you can—and should—add more detail than you normally would supply in the cramped boxes of most forms. Try to keep the descriptions or phrases brief. The chart comprises the raw information of your career database. In the next few exercises, new data and new columns will be added to this database as you add information about skills and outcomes. Eventually this database will include a column listing matching artifacts and career themes. The entire process will guide you in preparing your career portfolio.

► EXERCISE #6
Identifying Your Transferable, or Cross-Functional, Skills and Outcomes

With your basic experiences charted, now factor out the skills involved in each of them. Look at each job or learning experience and ask yourself, "What basic set of skills did I use to execute my duties/complete the learning?" Examine the building blocks—the many skills—that make up a job or learning accomplishment.

To better appreciate the creative act of skill-factoring, consider how it might be applied to a seemingly trivial artifact. Suppose, for instance, that you placed in your portfolio a list of your incoming e-mail. The employer chuckles and asks, "Why did you include this?" Can you list ten or more skills or talents represented by the e-mail listing? Try to take your thinking outside the conventional box and see how many skills you can identify. (Hint: Consider skills related to computers, professional development, networking, follow-up, research, and communication.)

In skill-factoring, you attempt to break down tasks and accomplishments into their constituent building blocks. To get to this molecular skill level, think in terms of discrete tasks and not the larger bundle of duties. As you try to describe the elemental skills, avoid using nouns or job titles like "locksmith." Instead use verbs or action phrases to describe what a locksmith really does. Use verb phrases to describe the fundamental tasks such as cutting keys, repairing or replacing broken locksets, rekeying locks, billing customers, advertising. To break these down further, look at the *what* and *how* of the job tasks.

EXERCISE #6 Continued

What tools are used? How are problems solved? When a locksmith approaches a new kind of lock, what research and communication skills are deployed? How does one handle the hysterical customer at the airport parking lot who called in a panic 30 minutes before boarding because his baggage was locked in the car? What methods are used to bill customers? In other words, how are the day-to-day tasks performed, and what skills are brought to bear on problem-solving situations?

Ask yourself, "What kinds of effort or actions actually went into my work?" How would you explain it to a middle-school student who is job-shadowing you for the day? How would you break it down so that the wide-eyed youth really grasps what it takes to do your job? The answers to these kinds of questions will help you to build a list of basic skills that are general enough to transfer from one kind of job to another.

For another example, suppose you spent the last three months helping your laboratory supervisor prepare for the impact of a reduced budget. You drew up detailed plans for a transition to a smaller laboratory. When the change was finally completed, you were "re-warded" with a severance package and an appointment with an outplacement counselor.

The feelings of betrayal and helplessness, anger and shame naturally took over and displaced your normally pleasant demeanor. You know that you can't begin job hunting until you somehow get beyond these dark emotions. To help realign your outlook, consider the skills involved in the immediate, complex task of restructuring and reducing the lab. My list begins with phrases like researched vendors, evaluated financing vs. lend-lease options, reviewed consumer reports, negotiated with supervisors, organized storage and sales. What could you add to the list?

The skill-factoring process involves looking beyond the technical terms. Consider, for instance, the financial controller in a corporation who lists a main job duty as *financial management.* This term fails to illuminate the skills behind this specialized task. The controller's duties could include *analyzing costs, planning budgets,* and *evaluating capital expenditures.* Notice these verb phrases sometimes end with "-ing" and describe the *what* or *how* involved in *financial management.*

Australian career counselor and author Paul Stevens finds that once his clients begin this type of skill-factoring, many are able to identify seventy or more skills within a week. In his book *Beating Job Burnout,* Stevens points out that the average person actually possesses several hundred skills when the term *skill* is defined loosely as anything one does well.

Before embarking on the skill-factoring exercise, it must be pointed out that the process should not be construed to mean that a general skill can be transferred to any job or become a substitute for a specific technical talent required for a particular type of work. You cannot apply for a position as a social scientist that requires applying statistical analysis to demographic data simply because you demonstrated general research skills while investigating lab equipment. But then, why would you apply for the sociologist's job unless you had some other assets and interests related to that type of work? A balanced approach recognizes the need to prove both general or transferable skills as well as specialized expertise or technical prowess.

As with a financial portfolio, it's important to periodically examine your assets in your career portfolio. You need to look not only at the diversity of your talents but also at the value of your experiences. You listed your assets in the Lifework Database in Exercise #5. These can now be expanded by factoring out transferable skills and your accomplishments or outcomes. (Later, you'll apply this analysis to the artifacts collected in your portfolio.)

1. Return to the chart you created in Exercise #5. Add a third column called *Skill Components*. Try to identify the constituent elements or skills that went into a given duty or responsibility such as *converting and downscaling the lab*. This means adding new words, typically action phrases and verbs. This new column constitutes your general and transferable skills that can be used on a variety of jobs. The general or transferable skills that might be found in the laboratory worker example could include the following: *researched, evaluated, reviewed reports, negotiated, organized, sold.*

   If you need some starter ideas or words, consult the word list in Appendix C: Skill Words. If you're still stumped, ask someone who knows you well to help. Show him or her the major duties you have listed and then ask the person to guess at the kinds of abilities or skills needed to complete the task.

   (Note: The example shown on the next page is only a partially illustrated chart. Each separate time period, such as 1992–1996 in the chart, could include several more items, perhaps fill a full page.)

2. There is one more vein to mine in your portfolio of experiences: your accomplishments or outcomes. Employers not only want to know what you did, but they also want to know how well you performed. In other words, what were the results or outcomes of your efforts?

   With skills factored out in the third column, now focus on describing the results of your efforts in a fourth column titled Outcomes. In a job search, descriptors represent qualities and accomplishments that can prove decisive in getting the job you want.

   Your most impressive outcomes are generally associated with your maximum efforts and peak moments. Try to recall those times when you tapped into a hidden energy source or special strength. These are the times when you literally lost yourself in the task! Such projects usually take countless extra hours or far more time than you originally anticipated. Additionally, these moments of excellence are usually associated with recognition, compliments, awards, and many thank-yous. Clues may come from people at work. How would your present or former colleagues complete the phrases: "We really miss your _____ abilities," or "Remember that time when nobody else could _____ and you came up with _____?"

   Stop looking at past experiences only in terms of money or time, and think instead of outcomes and results. Move away from thinking about how long you've been managing specialized projects, the number of years you've spent practicing

EXERCISE #6 Continued

law or teaching, or the number of college degrees you've earned; and move toward the tangible results of your efforts. How did you save money, time, or wear and tear? What did you speed up or make more efficient? Why did people give you more responsibility? Why did you receive an award or mention in an article? Why do people contact you on-line for advice? How did you use opportunities to develop your talents; in what forms of formal education and self-learning do you engage?

3. Finally, consider the portfolio-planning question. How could you prove some of the claims made in the last two right-hand columns? What artifacts or work samples could you collect? You can begin to brainstorm ideas by revisiting the list in Appendix B: Suggestions for Professional Portfolios. Don't worry about not having saved items. In the next chapter you'll learn how to creatively manufacture symbolic artifacts.

EXPANDING YOUR VIEW OF YOURSELF

As you complete the skill-factoring exercise, you may have begun to realize additional benefits of this self-assessment process. Too often, we take for granted the immensely satisfying "work" we do during leisure hours. For instance, if one enjoys photography, the typical response is to downplay it by saying something like "It's not work, it's easy; besides I enjoy it." Because you have taken the time to expand your awareness of talents or skills, you are less likely to become a victim of false modesty that prevents people from fully articulating all of their abilities. By creating a rich database of skills and talents, you will find it easier to describe your experiences on paper and during interviews.

Using the Database to Cope with Job Loss Trauma

If you have ever lost a job or been fired, you know that the aftermath feelings can be poisonous. You try to keep a lid on your feelings and make an effort to put the job loss in perspective, but you may find it difficult to discuss your last job with new employers. In the brief and constraining space of a job application or résumé, you simply write, "I helped convert and downscale our lab." Sorry, but that short line just may not be enough to land you a job interview.

You can't let negative attitudes get in your way when you compete for jobs. Return to the Lifework Database, drink deeply from this reservoir, brimming with your potential. As you do, your eyes will open to new possibilities—you may even regain your sense of humor. And, until you completely "heal," keep reading the funnies.

Lifework Database (expanded)

Time, Place, and Position	Major Duties or Responsibilities	Skill Components (Skill Factoring)	Outcomes (Peak moments, recognition, proof of excellence, improvements, and changes that benefited the organization)
1992–1996 LMN Inc. Community Rep and Training Coordinator	Promoted positive image in community Reviewed environmental impact statements Designed staff training	Wrote company newsletter, articles for paper Used a desktop publishing computer system Learned public-speaking skills Interpreted rules and regulations Assessed training needs, recruited and selected trainers Wrote and designed training materials	Asked to do a column on other topics Became regularly featured noon speaker Trainers always received good reviews Requests for training materials came from all over the country
1988–1992 College TSCE Student	Majored in Business Management and Training Involved in student clubs Helped set up a mentor program	Earned a 3.7 GPA Self-discipline, ability to learn a new trade Elected to president of the Student Business Roundtable Designed and coordinated a student mentor program (required outreach and marketing skills)	Outstanding Student Award from Rotary Club Made valuable business contacts that later assisted in my job at LMN The mentor program is still going, I have been asked to continue advising it

▶ # EXERCISE #7
Connecting Artifacts to Your Skills and Outcomes

Sometimes, instead of studying a list of words, try examining your portfolio artifacts with your eyes, hands, and mind. For kinesthetic, tactile, and right-brained learners, this approach may be an excellent alternative to working with word lists. Instead of analyzing and factoring skills from a list of words, try doing the same thing with the real-life objects in your portfolio. Even if you prefer words and data, handling objects will stimulate further thinking about skill-factoring.

Let's return to the earlier example of the person designing a new, smaller laboratory. Suppose this job seeker got permission from his employer to include a printout for the new lab's budget in his final portfolio. As the person fingers the printout, certain memories flood back about the day he stood by the printer, surveying the lab that might soon disappear. In this fashion, the normally mute artifact comes to life as it triggers a stream of feelings and words in the mind of the portfolio creator. Some of the words could be used later in a caption describing the budget printout. These words might also find another use when the interviewer asks, "Tell me about your last job." (Writing captions is discussed in chapter 9.)

One of Sara's Artifacts
Sara, a Portland, Oregon, chef, received a thank-you note from one of the restaurant's customers. Chefs don't get many written notes, so she tucked it into her bureau drawer. When the restaurant changed owners, Sara went looking for a new job. She used the letter shown on the next page in her portfolio as evidence of her attention to detail and customer needs. It proves she develops repeat business.

As you review Sara's letter, consider the kinds of skills she might factor out and possibly mention in a caption below the letter. To enrich the descriptions of your own skills, look over the words in Appendix D: Personality Words. You can use this list to help identify more words you can add to Sara's list.

Jerome's Artifacts
Jerome works in customer service in a software company. He operates the complaint line that is euphemistically referred to as the "customer satisfaction center." The bane of his existence revolves around the fact that products are periodically released before they are completely debugged. You can imagine the fun calls that come in from customers who upgrade and then can't operate their computers due to software conflicts. Near Jerome's phone is a bottle of antacid,

---

Artifact #1

Skills hidden in a simple thank-you note

Dear Chef,

My husband and I were here to celebrate our twenty-fifth wedding anniversary, and I want to thank you for making this a very special occasion. Normally, he is a very fussy eater and can only tolerate certain foods, so I knew that coming to your gourmet restaurant would be a challenge. Our waitress not only attended to my husband's every need, but she also went out of her way to make sure our special menu requests were attended to in the kitchen. I can only imagine what it must be like cooking all those meals. I wondered how you found the time to make a Caesar salad dressing without a raw egg, remove the raisins from the duck sausage, and siphon off the honey glaze from the dessert. Please accept my many thanks and the enclosed token for making this special night a memorable one.

Sincerely yours,

Judith M.

---

which was given to him by his supervisor during his first week on the job, three years ago. Several other phone jocks haven't lasted as long as his bottle of stomach medicine. Jerome always finds that two ingredients work best in fielding complaints: humor and follow-through. As a result, he receives more than his share of compliments, which are reported in his performance evaluations.

He is now creating a portfolio for his next evaluation and plans to use it when requesting a promotion or a raise. What skills could he factor out from this artifact? What stood behind the secret of the 3-year-old antacid bottle? To answer these questions, Jerome expanded the previous chart to include a column for artifacts. After factoring out skills and outcomes, he began listing the evidence or artifacts that help prove the skills and talents he is claiming.

The sample chart on the next page continues the process used in the earlier Lifework Database chart. If you are developing your own chart, this is the time to try to add a column of artifacts. To help you, keep in mind the following.

People are often valued at work for a combination of three types of skills that include:

Lifework Database

Major Duties or Responsibilities	Skill Components (Skill Factoring) & Outcomes	Artifacts
Listened to complaint and separated valid from invalid perceptions	Consistent communication Active listening Demonstrated patience and tough-mindedness Outcome Cooled down customer	Sample dialogue or recording of a phone call
Researched process of replacement or refund when product is beyond warranty date	Follow-up Negotiation Customer service Policy development Outcome New policy created for returning items overnight to residences	Policy statement
Researched how to send an overnight return from residence	Research, problem solving, planning Outcome Determined length of time needed for turnaround	Flowchart for shipping
Handled second complaint about length of time it takes to get a refund	Perseverance Outcome Retained as future customer Maintain sales volume	Pie chart showing fewer returned items
Received letter of praise from the customer Showed letter to boss, asked to train others	Training Outcome Received favorable mention in my annual review Asked to train others Increased responsibility	Letter of commendation Revised job description

1. Specific or technical skills. Pick artifacts that demonstrate specialized skills that are often associated with technical jargon and key words such as *corporate controller*.

2. General or transferable skills testifying to your general or transferable talents. These skills help you learn and prosper on any job. A more general skill would be budgeting.

3. Work habits or character traits. Choose work samples that demonstrate flexibility and versatility and other positive personality factors. Consider how you might illustrate personal qualities described by words like *enterprising, cooperative, self-disciplined, considerate,* or *self-directed*.

▶ # EXERCISE #8
Looking at Work Thematically

Thinking about your lifework in terms of themes provides you with a fresh, new perspective. In this exercise, you'll search for your life's "song" or the leitmotiv that animates the spirit of your work. Themes often describe long-standing interests, work styles, and preferences, no matter what task prevails in the moment.

In the book *Imagine Loving Your Work*, Marti Chaney describes a theme as the essence of your gifts, the qualities that have served you well in challenging moments. It represents a pattern or way you go about living and solving problems. Chaney suggests you think of single words that describe the one essential quality or activity you can't bear to live without. Oftentimes, these words end with either *-er, -or,* or *-ist: creator, promoter, teacher, risk-taker, explorer, optimist, facilitator, humorist*.

To get you started, think of how you would enjoy being toasted at a retirement or graduation party. Or how you'd like to be remembered in your epitaph. Each major theme can then be broken down into subthemes, just as job duties can be broken down into skills.

1. Review the Lifework Database chart in Exercise #6: Identify Your Transferable, or Cross-Functional, Skills and Outcomes. Add a new column at the far right to describe possible subthemes. As you look across a given row, search for a word or phrase that sums up the essential nature of the information, your character, or the main traits and talents presented here.

   Most people find it is best to start with their earliest experience because it's easy to think of a theme for a period separated by time from the present moment. If thinking thematically about your life is new to you, try Exercise #4: The Party Game in chapter 2.

2. A master theme, which can be built from the list of subthemes, could become the title for your portfolio. Assuming you had to label the entire chart with a single master title, what would it be? What seems to guide your entire lifework? Generally, you'll concentrate on

EXERCISE #8 Continued

the most recent part of the chart as you try to sum up where you are now or how you got to where you are today. A brief thematic title is often well-served by a slightly lengthier, more descriptive subtitle. In the previous Lifework Database chart example, the author used the phrase *Reaching Beyond Everyday Constraints* as a starting point and turned it into the statement *Daring To Step Beyond* to express the master title theme in her life. She also used a supporting theme as a subtitle. She began with a subtheme, *The Story of Communicating Possibilities in Tough Times*. Later, this evolved into an entire portfolio section entitled *Skillful and Tough-Minded Communicator*.

Later, you may choose to organize your portfolio by the various themes and subthemes. Thinking thematically can pay off, especially if you are asked to describe yourself in general terms at the interview. It might come in handy when you are asked, "How do you think others perceive you?"

Lifework Database

Time and Places	Major Duties or Responsibilities	Skill Components (Skill-Factoring)	Out-comes	Subthemes Possibilities
1978–1988 OHD High School	Depart. Head Develop program goals Teacher-Soc Stud	Communication skills, run meetings Human relations Teach 100 teens a day! (whew)	Many requests to see/tour department Turned an average dept into model one	Communicator Reaching Beyond Everyday Constraints
1988–1992 College TSCE	Majored in Business Management and Training Involved in student clubs Helped set up a mentor program	Earned a 3.7 GPA Self-discipline, ability to learn a new trade Elected to president of the Student Business Roundtable Designed and coordinated a student mentor program, required outreach and marketing skills	Outstanding Student Award from Rotary Club Made valuable business contacts that later assisted in my job at LMN Mentor program is still going, asked to continue advising it	Emerging Leader Self-discipline and Reward Mentor and Learner Innovating Realist

► EXERCISE #9
Using Your Ideal Job to Conceptualize New Possibilities

Don't become too attached to your job title; in today's dynamic workplace there's a good likelihood that it will change. Even if it doesn't, you're limiting yourself by thinking in terms of a specific job title. Instead, visualize fictional job titles related to your collection of artifacts and give yourself permission to begin making important connections and seeing new possibilities.

To get closer to alternative and possible new job titles, answer the next three questions as quickly as you can. Do this spontaneously so that you don't lose the impact of the questions.

1. Assume the local community college just received a funding cut. The administrators want to maintain their adult evening enrichment program. The school is soliciting community members for the purpose of providing instruction on something citizens might enjoy doing. What course could you possibly enjoy teaching at the college?

2. When thinking about our career choices, all of us have at one time or another said, "If I had to do it all over, I might have tried _____." Suppose you received a special "Starting-Over Grant" for returning to school. It would pay for all of your living and schooling expenses (including current debt obligations). What area might you choose to study if you could start all over?

3. Can you get excited about an ideal job that would combine some of your most unique talents? The job would be so much fun that it would not seem like work most of the time. It can be as wild as you want. It should be a job that combines skills that you have enjoyed using at different times or in different roles, including student, employee, hobbyist, volunteer, and any other oddball task you've enjoyed. Give this dream job a title—be inventive! For example, if you liked backpacking and writing, then you think about an *outdoor roving magazine editor*. List five made-up occupational titles describing your ideal job. Consult the Lifework Database chart you prepared in Exercise #8 for your list of talents and choose your favorites.

I enjoy journal writing, counseling others, using computers, studying job-finding strategies, and leisure wellness. The titles I came up with when I did this exercise were: *journal counselor, journal therapist, desktop publishing consultant, leisure counselor, matchmaker, leisure or job-search counselor, database coordinator, recreation therapist, desktop publishing teacher, computer artist.*

REALITY TESTING AND ADAPTING IDEAL JOB TITLES

Just because your ideal job cannot be found in the *Dictionary of Occupational Titles* or the local want ads does not mean the work does not exist! Each month, many one-of-a-kind jobs are created. There may even be an existing job that comes close to what you would like to do, but it uses an outdated (or misleading) job title from the past.

Therefore, your next task is to meet as many people as you can and ask them to help you locate something approximating your ideal job. Your enthusiasm will motivate people to help you. To give your dream job a reality test, begin by preparing a very simple portfolio that includes up to five artifacts related to one of your ideal, fictionalized job titles. You might include a simple cover with a title like *Possibilities?* Show this collection to people you know or people who may know something about the job market in your area. Ask them these three questions:

1. Please take a brief look at these samples that show what I really enjoy doing and do well. Can you tell me about any places or people who might share two or more of my interests?

2. Do you know anyone who is paid to use these kinds of talents?

3. Can you suggest anyone else I might talk with?

With any luck, you'll learn about people who might share your interests and passions. The people you meet in this manner can become invaluable in advising you further about your career choice, your portfolio, and job hunt. Once you connect with such people, they will often let you know about openings when they learn of them.

Sum up such networking by creating a list of possible places and people to visit in the future. If you are looking for more job ideas, review the next section and Exercise #10, which illustrates a method for relating your portfolio artifacts to existing jobs.

CONNECTING PORTFOLIO ARTIFACTS TO EXISTING JOB OPTIONS

After you've begun collecting artifacts for your working career portfolio, you can look for clues that link the artifacts to various occupations in particular or to broad categories of work in general. (If you haven't begun collecting artifacts yet, consider those you could collect now and others you plan to get in the future.) To help in analyzing the "job content" of your artifacts, we'll adapt a system used by job experts to classify various occupations. In the next exercise, you'll use three categories based on a system devised by the Department of Labor during the 1930s that still proves useful with job descriptions of today.

This system, designed to match job seekers with employers, codifies and describes job duties and skills in more than 20,000 jobs. The results have been compiled in the large *Dictionary of Occupational Titles* (abbreviated by career counselors as the *DOT*). Jobs in the *DOT* are arranged under one of nine major occupational categories. These can be cross-referenced to various types of businesses. The *DOT* also includes cross-references connecting military to civilian job titles.

Each job is coded with a lengthy nine-digit Occupational Code Number (OCN). Three digits within this code represent the types of worker functions needed to carry out the job. These three digits are used to describe how each job uses skills related to working with data (D), people and animals (P), or things (T). This is often referred to as the DPT code. Generally, the higher the skill function, the lower the number. The skills, samples, and numbering system are shown below.

Data
0 **Synthesizing**—integrating ideas, developing concepts and knowledge base
1 **Coordinating**—setting sequence of operations, reporting events
2 **Analyzing**—evaluating data, presenting alternatives
3 **Compiling**—gathering, collecting, collating, classifying data, reporting
4 **Computing**—mathematical or work with numbers, following plans carefully
5 **Comparing**—observing information and connecting ideas
6 **Copying**—transferring, entering data

People
0 **Mentoring**—counseling, resolving conflicts, advising (spiritual, legal, political)
1 **Negotiating**—exchanging ideas, formulating policies, reaching a consensus
2 **Instructing**—teaching, demonstrating, making recommendations
3 **Supervising**—guiding a group, developing teamwork, promoting efficiency
4 **Diverting**—amusing or entertaining others
5 **Persuading**—selling, debating
6 **Speaking**—signaling, talking, giving assignments or directions
7 **Serving**—attending to the needs or requests of people or animals
8 **Taking Instruction**—following directions

Things
0 **Setting up**—setting or adjusting equipment, altering jigs, fixtures, parts, repair
1 **Precision working**—selecting tools, guide materials for precision outcomes, adjusting tool to the task
2 **Operating/Controlling**—starting and stopping machines, fabricating mass or custom items
3 **Driving**—operating all kinds of vehicles
4 **Manipulating**—using some judgment to make items to standard specifications, adjusting materials or machine controls

5   **Tending**—tending, adjusting, or controlling semiautomatic equipment or processes
6   **Feeding/Offbearing**—supplying material to automatic machines
7   **Handling**—carrying or moving things, following standards

Anyone can use this coding system to help analyze the contents of a portfolio. You can consider each work sample in terms of skills and knowledge. Then try to relate these skills to working with data, people, and things. If you already know the job you want, you can look up the skills and experiences needed and then look for any gaps between what is needed on the job and what you have collected to-date in your portfolio.

To illustrate the process, consider a cook's job. One *DOT* rating for this job is shown below:

DPT Job Code	Data	People	Things
Cook (example code)	3 (average)	6 (low-average)	1 (high)

A cook uses a bit of data primarily in the form of recipes and orders (3), less appears to be needed in working with people (6), and most of the talents required relate to using equipment, tools, food, or what is generically referred to as "things" (1). Does this sound reasonable to you?

Compare this to a psychologist:

DPT Job Code	Data	People	Things
Psychologist	1	0	7

A typical psychologist must be able to analyze and coordinate data (1), be good with people (0), and have virtually no need to work with tools, machines, or "things" (7). Therefore, this job is rated with a 107. See if you agree with the following job ratings:

DPT Job Code	Data	People	Things
Reception Clerk	3	6	7
Dental Technician	3	8	1
Sales—Computer Parts	2	5	7
Sales—Art Supplies	2	5	1
Teacher of the Mentally Challenged	2	2	7
Teacher of the Physically Challenged	2	2	4

A reception clerk needs the ability to compile information or messages (3), speak with a variety of people (6), and rarely needs to work with things (7). A dental technician must be highly skilled at replacing crowns and bridges. And because this technician usually works alone at a bench, the job is given a 381 rating in the *Dictionary of Occupational Titles*.

Sometimes people who can do the same job but with different emphasis end up with slightly different scores. Selling in general is usually coded as a 357, but selling computers is a 257 (with greater emphasis on using more data), and selling art products becomes a 251 (that denotes the greater involvement in materials or things).

If you are a special-education teacher working with students who are mentally challenged, your code is 227, but if you work with physically challenged students your code is 224 because you need to know about wheelchairs, catheters, and other forms of support equipment. However, if you teach drama, then your code becomes 027, reflecting your involvement with literature and acting.

There are many ways to describe a job since no two jobs are ever performed exactly alike. You might not always agree with each DPT score because your work experience or knowledge of your job is unique to your setting or work history. But the DPT scores do show the skills that are generally needed on the job. As you can see, most jobs typically require the use of all three skills, with one or two skills emphasized.

► EXERCISE #10
Analyzing Portfolio Artifacts Using Occupational Codes (DPT)

What skills are represented in your portfolio? Which talents do you enjoy using most often: Data, People, or Things? You can use a DPT system of analysis to determine the "occupational story" contained in your portfolio.

1. Make a list of the samples in your portfolio (or the ones you plan to collect). After each item create a Data, People, Things code. Since this is your own assessment, only your opinion matters, and you don't need to check it against the *Dictionary of Occupational Titles*. A sample chart might look like this:

DPT Job Code	Data	People	Things
Artifact #1-Newsletter emphasizing both my editing and design skills. (Mastery of communication and information as well as working with desktop publishing software and hardware results in a high rating for Data and Things.)	1	4	2

EXERCISE #10 Continued

DPT Job Code	Data	People	Things
Artifact #2-Certificate of appreciation for chairing the committee on staff wellness. (Since this involves people skills and some management of information, Data and People received the highest rating.)	2	1	7

2. When you are done, determine which areas mattered most. Which one or two columns contain your greatest strengths (i.e., your lowest totals)?

3. What conclusion can you draw from your chart? Hopefully, the chart accurately reflects your experiences and interests. It is very important to examine the contents of your portfolio in light of the job you are seeking. Do the artifacts support your current career goal or job-search target? If they don't you have two options: collect more artifacts or reevaluate your goals and interests.

4. After considering your artifacts and DPT codes, you'll want to begin either looking for general information about jobs related to your experiences and interests, or gathering detailed background information about particular occupations. You can use your self-made DPT three-digit code to compare against jobs you find in other occupational references. This may help you evaluate the job according to your interests and aptitudes.

The goal in this exercise is not to brand you with a single job title, but rather to use the traditional job title codes as a creative tool. Remember, you don't have to worry about fitting yourself with the correct label or job title at this moment. This is especially true today when companies emphasize experiences gained on teams and projects and focus less on traditional job titles and departmental hierarchies.

Additional Occupational References

If you are considering changing your career direction, then you'll probably find it helpful to locate resources that group jobs by common aptitudes, duties, and skills. This way, you can compare your set of experiences, skills, and interests represented by groups of artifacts with a group of related occupations. An excellent starting resource is *The Complete Guide for Occupational Exploration (CGOE)* and the shorter version *The Guide for Occupational Exploration (GOE)* that classify jobs into twelve Interest Areas and sixty-six Work Groups with references to over 12,000 specific job titles. The *GOE* also shows you how to match your interests, values, experiences, studies, work experiences, and military occupational specialties to related Work Groups. After you find a Work Group compatible with your interests and experiences, you can then explore specific job titles that are further cross-referenced by *DOT* numbers.

Armed with a list of potential occupations, head for the index in the back of the *DOT*, which includes over 20,000 job titles. Feast upon the *DOT* smorgasbord. Browse jobs listed on pages before and after your specific job title because you may find something of interest in a related job title. The *Enhanced Guide for Occupational Exploration (EGOE)* combines some of the best features of the *DOT* and *GOE*. This reference limits its scope to 2,500 jobs representing approximately 95 percent of the people working today. The *EGOE* also includes *DOT* job descriptions. You can use your DPT coding of artifacts to screen your job possibilities.

Over twenty years ago John Holland developed a system for relating job skills and jobs to six personality types. Since then, over 15 million people have used this system, *Self-Directed Search,* to identify new career directions and options. This easy-to-use inventory helps you identify your personality type, which can then be cross-referenced to a very useful dictionary listing over 12,000 DOT occupations called *Dictionary of Holland Occupational Codes.*

The highly introspective approach in *The Quick Job Hunting Map* (which can be found in Richard Bolles' book *What Color is Your Parachute?)* will help you conduct a comprehensive self-evaluation. Once complete, you'll be able to indentify your transferable skills, salary needs, values, and preferences for people, work settings, and tasks associated with your career goals.

To deepen your knowledge further about specific jobs, you'll want to make a trip to the library or the career center at a local college or employment agency. A reference librarian or career counselor can direct you to books, videos, and on-line resources featuring information about specific occupations. Often the titles of these works begin with words such as *Careers in . . . , Opportunities in . . .* or *Career Guide To . . . ,* or *The Top XYZ Jobs.*

TAKING YOUR PORTFOLIO ON INFORMATIONAL INTERVIEWS

An important part of researching your career options is talking with people who actually perform the work you'd like to do. This is often called informational interviewing, and this process is briefly touched on in this next section and more fully explained in a number of books, including Richard Bolle's *What Color Is Your Parachute?* (see Resources, near the back of this book).

The informational interview is a very simple concept. You visit with people to discover what they do for a living, what they like about it, and what advice they might have to offer you about their career fields. In this manner you collect firsthand up-to-date information that can help you to decide about the kind of

The New Digital Frontier in Occupational Information Systems

In our information society, citizens often suffer from too much rather than too little data. A virtual information cornucopia awaits the person who wants to learn about occupations, labor market trends, training, or learning opportunities. Unfortunately, the information is widely dispersed across a dizzying array of resources with names like *The Guide for Occupational Exploration, Occupational Outlook Handbook*, and *Dictionary of Occupational Titles*.

Fortunately, new computer technologies now make it possible to share, integrate, and distribute information quickly and inexpensively. This has fueled a movement to unify the disparate information now enshrouded in the jargon of various professions such as economists and labor experts, vocational instructors, and career counselors. One new model has come on the scene; this automated dictionary of occupational titles is known as O*Net.

O*Net is a comprehensive database system for collecting, organizing, describing, and disseminating data on job characteristics and worker attributes. It contains information describing the skills, knowledge, and abilities needed for different kinds of work. It also includes information about the context or environment in which work is done and the employment outlooks for each type of work. It is like an electronic *Dictionary of Occupational Titles*, only richer.

As this book goes to press, private vendors and government agencies are experimenting with different models for distributing this information. One of the largest undertakings is a federally coordinated project known as America's Job Bank, an electronic bridge between the job seeker and employer.

In the future, it will be possible to survey opportunities for work and learning from the home, office, or classroom. One will begin an electronic career coaching session by entering personal data, such as background about school accomplishments, learning styles, personal limitations, work-style preferences, and work experiences. The digital window will zoom across a landscape of new possibilities, bringing back information about "cross-job descriptors." This data will then link one's present position to suitable job alternatives within organizations.

A displaced or downsized employee will be able to explore new positions within his or her former industry or consider entirely new lines of work based on transferable skills. A placement specialist for disabled individuals could examine the physical or mental demands of a job, and if job duties exceed the client's capacities, then he could search for comparable jobs with different requirements. When one lacks the matching experience or technical skills, he or she will be given a listing of internships, training programs, and scholarships.

O*NET is still in its infancy, but its potential is enormous. We are witness to a time ripe with possibility for electronically transforming the way we gather information about ourselves, our work, and training opportunities.

work you might enjoy doing. This is very helpful when you are choosing a first career or making a career change. While conducting this interview, you can offer to share your portfolio. Feedback from people working in the field can be invaluable.

Some busy managers may not want to take the time, nor feel it is their job, to counsel people making career decisions. However, the people you want advice from at this stage should not be the hiring authorities or high-level managers. Instead, select people who perform the kind of work you think might relate to your portfolio of interests or people who enjoy sharing information. I believe that most people will respond to a call for advice. You may have to meet on their lunch hour or after work; or maybe over a cup of coffee. Most people enjoy being asked their opinion when they have the time. I have never had any problem surveying or interviewing people for research projects, jobs, or personal topics of interest.

You might warm up to the task by finding people to practice with. Perhaps you could conduct an informational interview with career counselors at college placement offices, résumé writing experts, vocational instructors, job placement specialists, job service staff at your local state employment office, your favorite teachers, and even friends.

Getting Feedback on Your Portfolio

Once you've developed a near-final job-search portfolio (as explained in Part II), network to find people who perform work or use skills similar to the kinds of talents demonstrated in your portfolio. If that is not possible, try meeting with someone who knows about specific jobs such as vocational instructors, career counselors, or human resources specialists. Ask them if you might have time for a 15-minute meeting for the purpose of reviewing your professional portfolio. Tell them you are looking for feedback and advice.

Show them your portfolio and ask, "These are samples of what I enjoy doing. Do any of these relate to the kind of work being done here?" Then solicit their opinion about your portfolio contents. You might inquire: "Which of my items do you feel are the most important samples and why?" When you leave, end by thanking them and then asking for advice about others who might be able to help out: "Do you know of anyone else who might know about this field or who might know others who do? I'd like to get at least three opinions."

Such meetings will help you decide which artifacts to include and what is important on the job; you may also get good suggestions for collecting additional work samples for your portfolio.

4

THE JOB SEARCH PORTFOLIO

Using a Portfolio in Job Hunting, Interviewing, and Self-Marketing

▶ How does a portfolio differ from a résumé? Can you combine the benefits of a résumé and a portfolio in a single document? What's the best way to introduce your portfolio at a job interview? What can you do to build confidence and polish your portfolio presentation skills? You'll find the answers to these and other questions in this chapter.

JOB HUNTING WITH PORTFOLIOS AT DIFFERENT STAGES OF THE HIRING PROCESS

A résumé is a short (usually one-page) document that summarizes your job skills and knowledge as well as your work and, sometimes, education history. It's an introduction, so to speak, a brief review of who you are and what you have to offer an employer. A portfolio is not a résumé, and it shouldn't normally take the place of one. Those persons involved in the hiring process are probably looking at several dozens—maybe even hundreds—of résumés in the early stages of filling a position. They want to deal with less paperwork, not more. No one wants to invest the time in looking at nor in returning a portfolio from someone they're not already seriously interested in considering.

In fact, some companies today have turned the task of reading résumés over to a computer scanner. If you find out the employer is using a scanner for screening résumés, don't waste a portfolio on it. It's probably best to submit a simple résumé, one without fancy formatting, in plain ASCII text. In this instance, it is critical that you use key words in your résumé that the computer is looking for. For instance, a computer scanning for a dental technician probably searches for key words like *crown* and *bridge*. People looking for upper-management positions need to select key words that ring bells for executive recruiters. Based on a 1995 survey of 1,200 executive-level search firms by David Opton of Exec-U-Net, people searching for upper-level management positions should include terms and phrases related to the following: *change agent, leadership, motivator, able to influence and persuade, build team commitment.*

Firms that use a scanner won't even be able to "read" any portfolio you send in because they won't be able to get it through their computer—unless, perhaps you've got it in an electronic form and send it on a disk or via the Internet. (See chapter 13 for a discussion of electronic portfolios.)

The personal nature of the portfolio suggests that it is something you share only with people who are truly interested in evaluating your potential and your possible fit with their organization. This usually takes place near the end of the job-search process when the applicants have been narrowed down to just a few and you've been invited to an interview.

In the early stages of a job search, employers are soliciting a large universe of people and, more often than not, they want a quick-read résumé so that they can determine whether you qualify for a more serious review later. They are looking for specific skills or experiences and without these, your résumé will appear to be flawed or mismatched in terms of the employer's needs. When you know your résumé will be read primarily by humans (not machines), you may want to personalize it by blending some of the best qualities of a portfolio and résumé.

PORTFOLIO-RÉSUMÉ HYBRIDS

You can create a hybrid document that's suited to this early screening process by combining the best of a portfolio and résumé. This portfolio-résumé hybrid (which should be no more than four pages long) is designed to be broadcast to a large audience of potential employers and contacts. Because you have to keep it short, you've got to carefully select those samples that will have the maximum impact in your field of work.

Two methods for organizing this hybrid résumé-portfolio are shown in Artifact #2. The first example uses actual work samples, including a sales chart. The second illustration uses a photomontage or photo-essay, illustrating different technical skills. Notice that both forms of the hybrid portfolio are brief, with good amounts of empty, or white, space. Each tries to emphasize technical skills or accomplishments. Like résumés, these hybrid documents are designed to be distributed widely (and not returned). The document model is designed for a quick 1- to 2-minute read.

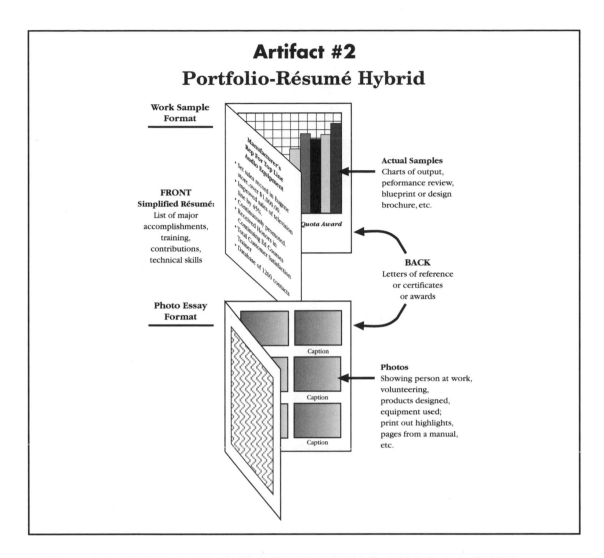

Artifact #2
Portfolio-Résumé Hybrid

Work Sample Format

FRONT Simplified Résumé: List of major accomplishments, training, contributions, technical skills

Manufacturer's Rep For Top Line Audio Equipment
• Set sales record in Eugene store: over $1,000.00.
• Improved sales of television line by 45%.
• Continuously promoted.
• Received Honors in Continuing Ed Courses.
• Total Customer Satisfaction Trainer.
• Database of 1200 contacts

Quota Award

Actual Samples Charts of output, peformance review, blueprint or design brochure, etc.

BACK Letters of reference or certificates or awards

Photo Essay Format

Caption

Caption

Caption

Photos Showing person at work, volunteering, products designed, equipment used; print out highlights, pages from a manual, etc.

NETWORKING AND DIRECT MAILING APPROACHES

If you are using networking to uncover potential jobs before they are advertised, then you're probably a step ahead of the competition. Every leading authority recommends making this your primary job hunting strategy, because up to 80 percent of the hiring on a given day is for jobs that are never advertised or at least not widely advertised.

In this book, networking simply refers to an exchange of information. It generally begins when you ask for help in locating people or information that can help you reach your job search goal. When you approach people, you should let them know that you value them and their backgrounds and that this is why you are asking for their help. If you build your relationship to a point of mutual respect, then they will be interested in helping you. Hopefully, they will offer you advice and support. They might also ask you questions such as "Where have you looked so far?" or "Have you thought about contacting XYZ?"

Cold Calling with Warm Portfolios

In addition to responding to job postings (in print and on-line) and networking to find leads, you can also do some direct contacting or "door knocking." In his book *How To Prepare Your Portfolio*, Ed Marquand advises art professionals and students to take a copy of their portfolios to agencies in order to leverage an interview. If you're unable to get an invitation to meet the hiring authority, Marquand advises, leave behind a copy as a calling card. This could be accompanied by a letter in which you request, "If my work fits into any immediate or future projects, please let me know. I'll check back with you next week."

Use Marquand's idea to spur your own thoughts about using your portfolio during cold calling. There are no rules for the nonartist job seeker. The subject of portfolios is wide open and being written by trailblazers such as yourself.

If they express a growing interest in your career and know something about your career field, then it is logical to consider sharing your portfolio with them at that point or some later time. If you impress them with your portfolio, they may be motivated to become active supporters in your job hunt and offer to keep their eyes open for any future leads. Then you have truly developed a quality network relationship.

THE INTERVIEW PORTFOLIO

Portfolios really come into play at the job interview—when you know that an employer is interested in you and wants to get to know you better and see what you've got to offer her organization. This is where you'll have your best opportunity to present your portfolio while you promote yourself.

Begin putting together your interview portfolio by culling the absolutely best examples of skills and abilities from your larger career portfolio. The final product should probably not exceed twenty-five pages, and shorter is often better.

The contents should include samples of technical competence and specific skills, as well as transferable and personality skills. For instance, if your job involves management skills, you might create a section on leadership, perhaps including a photo showing you moderating a quality circle or focus group meeting, a consultant's report about your strategy for improving staff moral and performance, or samples from strategic-planning charts. In a section on technical skills, you might include a sample print from the telecommunications project you coordinated or price forecasting graphs; a budgeting-skills section could feature charts and figures from a company report referring to your marketing accomplishments. In a section on your education, you might include transcripts from M.B.A. classes, samples of work you've had published in professional journals, or a list of presentations, professional citations, or performance evaluations.

The employer will be looking to see if you truly understand what the job demands and what the organization needs from its employees in your field and at your level. The person viewing your portfolio will consciously or unconsciously note how well your portfolio artifacts relate to his or her needs. If you've done your homework, it will show because your portfolio will be customized to the requirements of the job. It will demonstrate that you understand the skill standards, performance, and characteristics needed to make a contribution to this potential employer. This is something to keep in mind when creating your professional portfolio, especially in the process of artifact selection and display and overall design (these topics are covered in depth later in Part II).

Add the Personal Touch

Having been invited to interview, you can assume that you possess the prerequisite competencies required for the job. But so do the other people who've been asked to come in for interviews! At this next stage, many of the questions deal with issues of temperament, attitude, personality, or what interview experts call "fit." One job search expert compared it to dating. The job seeker and the interviewer size each other up and try to determine if the chemistry between them warrants a long-term relationship. This is where you want personality to come through. This is where the personal artifacts add a unique touch, making your portfolio shine.

Adding a personal touch to your portfolio will help round out a picture of your personality and temperament. Demonstrating people skills is always difficult since the area, by nature, is vague. If you're an executive, you could include lists of social organizations where you've made important contacts, such as charities, golf clubs, and cruises, as well as samples from your social circles. A letter, memo, or e-mail from a significant person in your industry that comments on some aspect of your personality or people skills could prove helpful. Consider adding a customer's thank-you note complimenting your diplomacy, the newsletter article mentioning your positive and enthusiastic attitude, or the photograph of the banquet where you were honored for loyalty and service (use a quote from the banquet speech as a caption for the article). If you think it's appropriate, demonstrate your sense of humor with the cartoon used in your last presentation on company policy.

It's a bit more challenging to demonstrate complex personality factors without going beyond the safe confines of traditional letters of reference. Intersperse these items throughout your portfolio to provide relief from the serious samples that document skills and accomplishments. (It's a good idea to get a second and even a third opinion regarding tastefulness and effectiveness of anything humorous or the least bit eccentric!)

The Portfolio Evens the Interview Playing Field

The job interview, the single most important part of the hiring process, is still, for the most part, highly subjective. Interviewing is not a science, but an art, and very few interviewers consistently pick winners.

Two Basic Types of Job Search Portfolios

Think of creating two different portfolios in your job search. In the beginning, when you are responding to specific job openings or broadcasting (cold calling), you can use a résumé-portfolio hybrid that emphasizes specific job skills (such as those found in Appendix C: Skill Words). Later, when you're preparing for a job interview, put together a more comprehensive portfolio. Be sure it includes samples of both specific skills and the more general personality traits (such as those found in Appendix D: Personality Words) so that your portfolio presents a well-rounded picture of yourself.

Hiring authorities know the scenario all too well. Quiet Quinellan shows up and sits demurely through the interview, offering thoughtful and slowly paced answers in her soft voice. She's followed by the exuberant Clever Cindy who immediately puts her inquisitors at ease with sophisticated humor and grace and offers up quick comebacks for any and all questions. Cindy, of course, gets the job. But later, her boss and coworkers find that Cindy is difficult to work with and lacks follow-through. She's all flash!

Looking back, we see that people are often chosen based on interview skills rather than work skills. Innumerable books provide all kinds of tricks to help one become smooth like Cindy. Entire chapters have been written about the art of small talk that precedes the interview. Readers are coached to scan the environment for clues about the employer's interests, calling this "room language."

You can look upon this situation from many different points of view, calling it manipulation, persuasive language, or survival. Regardless of your position, it is your behavior, up to and including the interview, that determines the final selection. Everything you do is judged: appearance, gestures, body language, verbal skills, résumé, and portfolio. The greater the effort put into preparation, usually the better the impression. A hastily constructed résumé is worse than not having one at all, and the same holds true for portfolios. You'll want to use every means at your disposal to tell the world "If I put this much work into my portfolio and presentation, imagine what I'll do for you on the job!"

If you achieve this level of performance, then your portfolio will definitely give you an edge during the interview. As you tell your story with the help of one, don't be surprised if you are asked to hand it over for closer inspection. Once your interviewers begin examining your portfolio, you are better able to guide the flow of the conversation in the direction of your talents. A portfolio can level the communication playing field because people who lack confidence in their impromptu verbal skills can walk in with a well-crafted portfolio that doubles as a script or interview aid. Perhaps in the future, our Quiet Quinellans will get more notice and the Clever Cindy will be evaluated on evidence rather than effervescence.

Injecting the Portfolio into the Interview Process

Prior to going in for the interview, use every means at your disposal to make sure your interviewers know that you have a portfolio. On your résumé and in correspondence, use a line such as "Professional portfolio available upon request." Mention your portfolio when you phone in your confirmation for the job interview. All of these pointers set the stage for showcasing your portfolio during the interview. Few employers will take the initiative and ask prospective candidates to bring in samples of their work.

Once at the interview, you'll need to look for opportunities to introduce your portfolio. If you are not formally asked to show it, use an interview question as an invitation. The query might sound like this: The interviewer asks, "Can you explain how you reduced the turnaround time for filing dates?" You reply, "Certainly. In fact, I've brought some samples of the final procedure sheet we used."

Use It to Show and Tell

If you prefer an indirect approach, you can simply ask if he'd like to see samples from your portfolio pertaining to the question. Should you want to be more direct, open up the portfolio to a specific section for your interviewer to see and describe the effort represented by your artifact. To make a stronger connection, remove your sample and hand it to your listener. Some portfolio authors mount each portfolio item on a matte board or laminate it so that they can quickly hand over any object they need rather than have to hunt for the sample in a bound version. And individual artifacts make it easy to alter the sequence of a presentation to fit the interview. Alternately, if your interviewer seems interested, consider handing the entire portfolio over to him.

When someone requests that you give an example of your ability to adapt to changing situations, they are probably probing for clues about your character or personality. Use this as an opportunity to bring up your last job evaluation, show photos of how you changed an office space to accommodate more staff and fewer resources, or present anything else related to your adaptability at a previous job.

If you are just out of school, you might be asked questions about statements on your résumé or application. For example, the interviewer might ask, "Your résumé states that you were an honor student in science." You respond with "Would you like to see the research paper that won special commendation? I have it here in my portfolio." Or she may say, "Tell me about the time you worked for the school newspaper." You then open up to sample articles or the school newspaper masthead listing your name as lead reporter. You're now off and running.

Any time you are asked for evidence or examples of how you perform on the job, think of it as a neon sign flashing: "It's show-and-tell time!" Bring out the portfolio, but limit yourself to just those samples that apply to the question. Never attempt to narrate your portfolio page by page. Keep your portfolio closed during most of the interview, using it only to help illustrate a point or demonstrate a particular skill or experience. However, don't be surprised if you get asked to leave your portfolio behind for examination. In fact, if you're interviewed by a panel of people, you may discover that some of the panel members will find the portfolio a pleasant diversion from the long hours of listening to applicants.

If in Doubt, Bring It

The interview process today often has many layers to it. Instead of just attending one interview, you may be asked to meet with an interview committee that then recommends finalists for an interview with decision makers. Other times, following an initial screening interview, the selected finalists will be invited to meet coworkers or department heads, put on a demonstration for peers, or go through one or two more additional interviews. If you find yourself in a rather lengthy or complex interview selection process, there will be no single correct time at which to introduce the portfolio. Your safest bet is to bring your portfolio with you at all times.

Since portfolios are a new concept for most people, it is hard to make absolute rules to cover every hiring situation. Take the case of one job seeker who reported bringing his portfolio to his first interview, which involved a panel. After getting his new appointment, he asked his boss, the vice chancellor of student affairs, about her reaction to his portfolio. She noted that the portfolio was interesting to see, but by the time he had been invited to the on-campus interview, her questions no longer concerned expertise but instead centered on his "fit" with the staff and campus. In retrospect, he felt that it might have made more sense to send out the portfolio to the initial committee charged with evaluating credentials rather than waiting until the on-campus interview, which dealt more with "match." However, his new supervisor did comment that she was glad to see that the work samples supported her perception that he would fit.

The Sale Begins When the Tough Questions Start

Sometimes, you may discover that your interviewer finds the portfolio samples so compelling that he leaves his preplanned questions behind and begins examining your material in detail. Consider the questions you might be asked. Typically, people want more details about a page that intrigues them. The questions often begin with the words, "How did you . . . ?" Or, the exhibit might remind the interviewer of a similar problem he needed to solve, and he asks, "What would you do if . . . ?" In such instances, he is actually visualizing you working for him, and he wants to see how you might fit in. Focus on the efforts, problem solving, or skills represented by the portfolio product. And never, never discuss past difficulties; avoid complaining or speaking negatively about any previous work situation or person.

You may also find that you'll get lots of "oohs" and "aahs" accompanied by a nod as the interviewer acknowledges the hard work represented by a particular work sample. He's been there and knows what it takes. Thoughtful interviewers will begin with general questions seeking background. They might ask, "Tell me how you established a consensus on this project." This will be followed by more probing in-depth inquiries: "What was the greatest challenge you faced in this event?" Astute observers will ask you to reflect upon the experience. They might query, "If you had to do this again, how might you approach it differently?" or "What did you learn about your strengths and limits from doing this task?"

All of the questions show an interest in learning more about you. They are a good sign because people about to make a major decision (like hiring someone) often start by asking difficult questions—they are trying to reassure themselves. It's an important point in the interview and is nicely summed up by the old sales axiom, "The sale doesn't begin until the customer objects." This means that when they begin asking tougher questions, you're moving closer to a "sale."

And you've got the answers, because you wrote the (portfolio) book!

Encore Performance

Even if you are not asked, you can offer to leave your portfolio behind once the interview is over. Leaving it will give you an excuse to pay your potential employer another visit. I personally like to return to the scene of the interview as soon as I can. Coming back to pick up the portfolio is a great opportunity to drop off a thank-you note, chat with the administrative assistant, or simply give everyone in the office another chance to see your bright, shiny face in their work place. You might even follow up with a short note thanking the interviewer for reviewing your portfolio and asking if he wouldn't mind sharing with you his reactions or suggestions about it. Were there any samples that matched the company's current projects or that he'd like more information about?

That said, never leave an original document with an employer or contact. High-quality, near-flawless copies of photographs, artwork, and color samples can now be created fairly inexpensively at copy and print shops.

Even If They Never Open It

Occasionally, job seekers have told me that they were never asked to show their portfolio and even their offer to leave it behind was spurned. In light of the time and effort you put into your portfolio, you may find yourself asking in this situation, "Was it worth it?" The answer is "Yes." Most job seekers felt better prepared for the interview and more able to field questions after having developed a portfolio. (People who carefully prepare their résumés only to find that they're not always read also feel they've benefited from writing them.)

PRESENTATION TIPS

Portfolios are mute documents, unable to speak for themselves. Composed primarily of artifacts and supported by a few lines of text here and there, they need your help to tell the full story with passion and insight. The contents of a personal portfolio are generally shared in a casual, warm, often humorous moment. Not so with a professional portfolio. It often requires a formal presentation.

The archiving, writing, and assembly of a portfolio is typically a solitary act. But all this changes once your portfolio is finished. As you go out to sell your story, you must take center stage. Some people are comfortable with this; and if you are one of them, perhaps this is the point at which you'll choose to close this chapter. If, on the other hand, you cringe at having to promote yourself, you're not alone.

In fact, in a list of the ten top personal fears among people in the United States, public speaking is right up there, along with fear of heights, death, loneliness, insects, and mad dogs. What would be your worst fear about presenting your portfolio? Look over the following list and pick those that best describe you:

- "I'll be inarticulate or nervous. I'll lose my advantage."

- "I'll get confused or appear disorganized when I lose my place."

- "I might get asked a question I can't answer."

To move beyond these fears and feelings, keep reading.

Techniques for Coping with Performance Anxiety

In *Book Blitz*, an excellent resource about selling one's writing, the authors help would-be promoters how to cope with performance anxiety during interviews and lectures. They tell the story of a shy author who broke down and confided to a nearby actor standing in the wings. She confessed feeling overwhelmed with the thought of stepping out on stage and talking to the faceless strangers sitting in the uniform rows. The seasoned thespian responded, "You're not nervous, you're just excited and filled with extra energy."

If left to itself or ignored, your extra energy finds its own avenue of expression, sometimes showing itself as fidgeting with a pencil, playing with a button, or a tapping a foot. The raw energy pours out of one's fingertips, neck, and feet. But if channeled correctly, nervous energy can be put to good use when presenting your portfolio. Handling the portfolio, turning pages, perhaps even standing to demonstrate a specific exhibit provides you with a chance to move around. It gives you a welcome outlet for your energy.

Your goal is to harness the energy to the best of your ability. Think of it this way: If you didn't possess this energy in the first place, it would be a sign that you don't care very much about the interview. Put this energy in perspective. Consider the following list of techniques and pick two or more of them to try when you prepare your next portfolio presentation.

Before the Interview
- To be truly effective in presenting your portfolio, you'll need to incorporate it into your interview preparations and rehearsals. Since the portfolio

involves a "show and tell," rehearse how you'll use it in your responses or possible interview questions. Carefully review both your portfolio and the job announcement before going to the interview in order to stay focused. Then practice answering questions you think you might be asked. As you answer, rehearse everything from referring to your portfolio and picking it up to thumbing through it to the page you need. Rehearse, rehearse, rehearse! Do it with friends and sympathetic listeners. Later, seek out opportunities to practice your presentation further. Try sharing it with teachers, peers in your field, even colleagues.

- Get plenty of sleep. Eat lightly. Drink lots of water. Visit the rest room before going to your appointment with destiny!

- Acknowledge your fears to yourself; give yourself permission to be anxious. (It's okay to admit that you're afraid, but don't share this with the audience.) Remind yourself that it's just energy. It can power fear or excitement. Try to make the best choice.

- Praise your own level of concern and your risk-taking spirit.

- Right before you enter the interview room, breathe deeply and slowly. Slow, even breathing has a calming effect.

During the Interview
- Call the interviewer(s) by name, if at all possible. This will put them at ease and create a personal link with them. We all like to hear our name.

- Don't try to be someone you are not. Don't mimic any interviewees who may have gone before you. Be yourself.

- If you get lost answering a question or giving an example, pause, take a deep breath, and adjust. Then continue after you collect yourself. I am constantly amazed at how harshly I grade myself during a lecture or workshop. The audience rarely notices one tenth of the mistakes I think I've made. Pause and then continue. This might make you look more relaxed and slow down an otherwise hurried answer.

THE MARKETING PORTFOLIO

Like a job search portfolio, a marketing portfolio has a very targeted use—to promote you, not to prospective employers, but to people who might buy your services or products or support your business in some way. It may be just the ticket for selling your ideas to bottom-line thinkers: financial backers, potential partners, funding organizations, or customers. It's an excellent tool for focusing your business goals, communicating your vision, and marketing your business,

---

It Has to Look Professional

A portfolio intended for marketing must possess the eye appeal and visual qualities of a professional brochure. The design principles in chapter 11 will get you started and give you the basics. Do a rough draft yourself first, then take your mock-up to a professional designer or advertising agency for the final production. You can save yourself valuable consulting time (and money) this way.

---

services, or products. Portfolios have been included in applications for business loans and grants and as adjuncts to consulting projects. Your audience might be a customer, executive, or a review panel—and they all need to be convinced that you are worth the investment. Persuasion is the essence of marketing, and portfolios are excellent persuaders.

Looking for Start-Up Loans

Students enrolled in an early childhood care program were asked by their teacher to compile a portfolio that not only reflected their studies but also their knowledge of the child-care industry practices. The students were required to interview local employers to increase their awareness of the business operations. When completed, their portfolios contained samples of specific skills such as lessons plans, instructional resources, and discipline policies. In addition, they included floor plans, staffing outlines, and start-up budgets. Two of the more ambitious graduates walked into their local bank with portfolios and plans in hand and left with a small business loan to help start up a business of their own!

Securing Grants

In addition to investment in for-profit entities, a large stream of investment dollars flows into the "independent sector" or nonprofit agencies. This often comes in the form of grants. Many grant proposals are written in dry or academic terms and could use a little dressing up. After staring at a large stack of text-laden and jargon-heavy grant proposals, the weary grant evaluator will welcome the stimulation and visual appeal of a portfolio document.

One community-oriented person I know developed a unique gardening service for low-income families while completing studies in urban renewal. The service used donated materials and technical expertise to help these families grow foodstuffs to supplement their diets while introducing them to the joys of working in a garden. A supporter from a local agency suggested, "Why don't you try getting a grant so you can do this full-time?" Eventually, the community gardener applied for a grant to extend the project to a larger, countywide scale. The proposal contained a project portfolio illustrating the different steps used in client outreach, donation solicitation, seed preparation, and the actual training and implementation conducted on the multiunit dwelling sites.

Marketing To Customers

An interior decorator meets with a client and brings exhibits showing before and after pictures that demonstrate how his decorating magic has turned mundane bedrooms and living rooms into rooms with real style. A landscaper looking for a loan brings pictures of residences and businesses where she has created tree-lined patios and set in beach-pebble pathways. In both cases, the portfolio becomes a convincing self-marketing tool.

This type of marketing portfolio must focus on the products or services and end with documents that can help you close the sale. It often begins with pictures that show problems you've come up against in the past or that draw a parallel between your current prospective client or customer and a past customer with similar needs. Then it shows the solutions or benefits of using your services. Finally, it might include sample contracts, menus of services, or pricing lists.

5

THE CAREER ADVANCEMENT PORTFOLIO

Using a Portfolio in Performance Reviews and for Raises and Promotions

▶ Using a portfolio during the job search is only half the story. Maintaining your collection once on the job is the other half of the portfolio mind-set. Adding new material to your working career portfolio, archiving as you go, helps keep your career in a state of constant readiness. As a result, you'll be prepared for any sudden moves, including moving out (after downsizing), moving laterally (to a new position or after a merger), or moving up.

Another reason for maintaining your portfolio on the job has to do with the fact that employers are now exploring new methods for evaluating, preparing, and rewarding employees. In some forward-thinking companies, employee evaluation and development fall under banners marked *succession planning, competency-based management,* and *gap analysis*. These terms, each of which could be a book in itself, are about new ways to help people prosper on the job and plan for their career development. And employees who use a portfolio to plan their careers and their lifelong learning take on the attributes most sought today. In business parlance, an employee with a portfolio appears to be headed for "high performance" and "active learning."

PREPARING FOR PROMOTIONS AND EVALUATIONS

When you head in for your performance evaluation, don't rely on your manager, mentor, or department head to recall your efforts and contributions. Even if you have a good relationship with your supervisor, he or she may not be around during the next cycle of employee reviews and promotions. Who, then, will recall the extra hours you put in to finish that big project for the new client? The evenings in August you stayed late because vacation schedules left the office understaffed? How you trained four new staffers and brought them up to speed in record time?

Did you remember to document your accomplishments?

Career experts have long advised employees to collect evidence of their performance to support requests for promotions or raises: save the memo that mentions your extraordinary efforts, keep a copy of the report later cited in the boardroom, archive the brochure you designed or the survey you worked on to assess company culture and wellness policies.

When there is no official document, learn to become your own data gatekeeper. Log the hours of overtime you put in, keep a record of the committees you serve on, compile a list of the dates and names of conferences and seminars attended. Tabulate the number of phone calls you handle, cases processed or closed, transactions completed, voice messages and e-mail answered each day. Create a graph or pictorial representation of the people reporting to you or your volume of sales. Write a synopsis of special projects you worked on or new courses or self-study programs you pursued.

PREPARING FOR LATERAL CHANGES

In today's flattened and streamlined corporate hierarchies, climbing the corporate career ladder seems beyond the grasp of many people. Most of us no longer look up—we look sideways. We think about ways to alter or expand our current job to better fit our goals and untapped talents.

If you enjoy training people, perhaps you can jettison your report-writing duties to someone else in exchange for setting up a mentoring program for new employees. Or, if you are hooked on computers, you could propose becoming the organization's Webmaster and offer to set and maintain its Web site. Maybe after enrolling in some classes about international trade relations, your proposal about establishing contacts abroad will be taken more seriously. Studying new communication techniques might result in you being given some management responsibilities. While not a promotion in the traditional sense, a change in your job description, like one of these above, could improve your overall job satisfaction.

Today's enlightened human resources departments recognize the value of helping employees manage and plan their careers. One large corporation, Motorola, has organized career-management centers that encourage the use of career portfolios in helping its employees plan career changes. And half way around the world, Paul Stevens, director of Australia's Worklife Centre, encourages people who feel a need for change or growth to approach their current employer with a formal proposal, perhaps packaged as a portfolio presentation, that describes a new way to execute their jobs.

Catherine Smith likes to compare portfolios to legal briefs. In her book-in-progress *Make Your Case*, she suggests that the exhibition-enriched nature of portfolios fits the promotional task at hand. When it comes time to ask for or defend your request for a promotion, a change, or an improvement in your compensation package, enter the discussion with your briefcase fully loaded. The portfolio process, when applied to employee evaluation, simply formalizes the process of communication and review and may improve the clarity of both the employer's and manager's mutual goals.

PORTFOLIOS OFFER PROMISE FOR NEW EMPLOYEE EVALUATION PROCEDURES

As we move out of rigid job descriptions and hierarchical departments and into more collaborative projects or teams, the nature of what we do and how we do it changes. Many of us are expected to use our talents with an ever-changing group of people and in a variety of projects, demanding that we possess both technical skills and people and team skills in order to succeed.

Consequently, the traditional method for assessing employee performance is also changing. Some businesses are experimenting with compensation packages that combine graduated increases in income with other incentives and bonuses. Pay raises—once based only on years of service or seniority—are today more often based on how much an individual contributes to the organization's bottom line, measured in terms of overall performance and outcomes on specific projects.

Instead of checking off little boxes or making brief comments on a laundry list of performance criteria at the end of the year, it would be far more useful to both employees and their managers if evaluations were done after each project. If the employee and his or her evaluator begin by jointly designing a rubric or evaluation guide pegged to specific goals or performance indicators, then they can begin the next cycle of assessment with a shared vision of what needs to be accomplished. In addition, the employee would know what documents to collect and bring to the next performance review. This method of evaluation is currently being used for many educators and by some government agencies (such as the Henrico County, Virginia government). Companies deploying workers in temporary positions and teams may find that the ongoing portfolio-based evaluation process helps them to creatively shape the attitudes and shared expectations of their workforce.

Creating a Rubric to Evaluate Job Performance

How might a performance evaluation be captured in a scoring rubric, and how could it reflect the outcomes on a specific project? There would be no job titles nor

Sample Performance Rubric

Criteria

3—<u>Professional Level</u>
Final polished work, competitive, effective, convincing evidence, matches work sought; exceeded expectations

2—<u>Working Level</u>
Generally convincing, good beginning draft or product, some discrepancies; met expectations

1—<u>Entry Level</u>
Acquiring knowledge, techniques, samples, artifacts, shows potential to meet expectations

Performance Outcomes (Tailored to a Specific Project)

_____ Completed training session about required product

_____ Developed survey items used in the customer-needs survey

_____ Uses effective communication and interpersonal skills on the team

_____ Executed research plan and collected usable data

_____ Met team deadline or project goals

Overall Performance Rating: _____

Areas of excellence:

Areas to improve or develop in:

specific job duties. Instead, assessment criteria tailored to a specific project would replace the standard boilerplate list found on most employee evaluation forms.

Suppose your company wanted to measure or document the performance of the participants in a customer-needs team. The members might be drawn from various parts of the organization where customers interact with the company or product. This team could include people working in sales, accounting, repairs, design, marketing, public relations, and message centers. Its mission could be to develop a method for continuously collecting data about customer satisfaction and needs and then feeding this information back to marketing and design teams. Later, this customer-needs team could be called back to assist in the design of a survey instrument that would be used in market research for a new product or service. At the end of the fictional project, employees could be evaluated on performance with a form resembling the one shown in the box here.

There are several advantages to thinking about your work in terms of rubrics and performance assessments. First, when you adopt the performance-evaluation framework, you learn how to view your portfolio from the same vantage point as an employer or supervisor. Also, thinking in rubric terms may help you remember to document and archive project and teamwork efforts. (In chapter 12, you can use the rubric evaluation method to assess your own portfolio.)

Whether or not your company uses these methods, you can still create your own rubric just as you create your own portfolio. You can then use both tools to reach a positive closure at the end of a project. For instance, before moving on to your next project, instead of requesting only a letter of reference, ask your supervisor to look over and rate your portfolio, perhaps even using your rubric. If nothing else, you'll get a bit more attention and are more likely to be remembered when the next big project needs talented self-directed people.

Benefits of Employee Portfolio Evaluation Systems

The portfolio evaluation can also help to simplify the exchange between the person(s) conducting performance reviews and the individual being assessed. The employee need only submit a portfolio containing evidence of what was learned, how skills were applied, and the level of competency achieved. This can be demonstrated with work samples, letters of appraisal, testimonials, and demonstrations.

As evaluators gain experience in assessing portfolio contents and portfolios themselves, they will develop criteria, models, and benchmarks that can guide them in rating and, ulti-

Portfolios Stimulate Growth and Renewal on the Job

David Beam is a political scientist at the Illinois Institute of Technology. His story illustrates the benefit of keeping your portfolio up to date and of getting into the archiving habit.

Dr. Beam was asked to submit a portfolio of his work for an evaluation that would determine his tenure status. Portfolios for college-level faculty typically include statements of teaching philosophy, teaching evaluations, articles, course syllabi, letters of reference, reviews of published books, citations of one's published works, evidence of community service, and notices of awards or special recognition. His final portfolio was presented in a large three-ring notebook divided into segments according to his university's criteria for promotion and tenure. He submitted publications—books and articles—in a separate box while his department chair collected confidential letters of reference that were added later. All of this was then reviewed by the university's promotion and tenure committee.

Dr. Beam felt enriched by the process of reviewing past accomplishments that had included work in government and business as well as academia. In reflecting on the experience, he commented, "It brought back memories of satisfactions that I had nearly forgotten because of the normal focus on today's job, today's projects, tomorrow's deadlines." Furthermore, Beam felt that the exercise gave him a somewhat different perspective on his interests and talents, one that "suggested some new ideas for research and writing."

With the new emphasis on self-directed and self-managed teams, one can speculate that sooner or later people in business might want to capture the same portfolio benefits experienced by those in academia. It is not hard to imagine that human resource professionals in increasing numbers will explore a portfolio system of self-evaluation that leads to a new kind of employee renewal.

mately, in comparing portfolios. The assessment process then becomes more accurate and more authentic because it relies on real-life artifacts rather than the one-dimensional paper and pencil tests. Likewise, the portfolio assessment process provides an alternative to promotions that are dictated by office politics.

6

THE LIFELONG LEARNING PORTFOLIO

Managing Your Learning Assets to Stay Competitive

▶ Economizing measures in organizations today often include downsizing as well as cutbacks in staff development and training. You can't rely on an employer for a long-term job, nor for the training needed to stay marketable. This means that you need to take charge of your own learning—and you need to document the skills and knowledge you acquire along the way. This may become especially important if you notice a gap between your current skill base and the new work you want to engage in next.

If you're not in school at this time, you would do well to heed the lessons of students and self-directed learners who are taking responsibility for designing and assessing their own learning. They know that the only real unemployment insurance is staying competitive by updating knowledge and upgrading skills. Each hour spent in formal learning or self-improvement is money in the bank. Lifelong learning is an asset that needs to be managed just as financial assets are managed.

Continuous Improvement = Lifelong Learning

The continuous growth and improvement of an organization is dependent on the continuous growth and improvement of its employees. Luckily, the many and varied educational pathways available today mean that almost everyone can find the time and means to learn, regardless of learning style or lifestyle.

Schooling oneself is not limited to textbooks or institutions. Many people pick up a skill through self-directed learning projects. Just think about how many people have taught themselves computer and Internet skills and all those who've turned a hobby into a marketable skill. And through distance learning

Relating School to Work with Portfolios

Thom Rakes was working as an assistant director in the Career Center at the University of Missouri when he began promoting both print and on-line portfolios. Rakes advises his graduates to take a portfolio along on their interviews. He encourages them to include samples from class projects, internships, cooperative work experience placements, summer and part-time jobs, volunteer work, and service learning opportunities. He believes that today's employers are looking for students who have both a degree and some work experience. Rakes is one of those rare experts who not only advises his students to use portfolios, he also puts that advice into practice himself and used his portfolio to pursue his next career move, as a career center director.

technologies, you can take individual courses and two-year, four-year, and even advanced-degree programs right in your own home, via TV, print material, videotape, audiotape, computer software, and the Internet.

A degree is important, but so is the education and training you receive after earning your degree, regardless of how or where you get it: in conventional classrooms, in professional seminars, by corresponding with instructors, by researching information on-line, in internships and volunteer activities, or on the job. As an active lifelong learner, one of your most important tasks is to keep track of your learning experiences. You can use your learning portfolio to document all forms of education and help you prove that your learning and self-improvement efforts relate to the work you seek or the promotion you desire.

MANAGING YOUR ASSETS WITH A LEARNING PORTFOLIO

The learning portfolio is like a revolving door that connects schooling to work. While in school, you can use your career portfolio (see chapter 3) to assess your strengths and interests. This information can help you plan long-term career goals that, in turn, can help shape your more immediate educational plans. If you are returning to school to upgrade a skill or retool in a new direction, then your previous portfolios can be used to document skills and knowledge that might earn you credit for prior learning and work experience. As you exit school, your new learning artifacts can be added to your job-search effort to demonstrate that you have acquired leading-edge knowledge and skills. Back and forth, from school-to-work-to-school-to-work, the portfolio becomes the vital connection between learning and working.

From Learning Portfolio to Professional Portfolio

From kindergarten through college, many students today are being asked to "show what they know" with portfolio samples. This is because educators have found that portfolios present a richer portrait of a student's growth, change, and reflection than standardized test scores and semester grades. A growing number of colleges are using portfolios, both in their classrooms for instructional purposes and in their career planning and placement centers. Students in such colleges are learning how to chronicle their development in a learning portfolio and then convert it into a professional portfolio prior to graduating so that they will have an effective job-search tool when they begin to look for work.

UNI's Experience

The Department of Curriculum and Instruction at the University of Northern Iowa (UNI) is one such school. It uses the portfolio both as an instructional tool and a professional job-seeking vehicle in its Early Childhood and Elementary Education program. Students are expected to produce four portfolios that accompany them through the transition from student to employee.

The first three portfolios are used to demonstrate growth and evaluate learning. For the most part, these portfolios contain samples from classwork, lesson plans, and field experiences. Students are asked to reflect on the meaning of their samples. As they review the contents, students address three critical questions: Why should I teach? How have I mastered my content and gained an understanding of children? What am I trying to do to grow or increase my effectiveness as an educator?

After collecting samples over four years, students find they own a treasure chest of artifacts. These working portfolios, sometimes called *folios*, might include photos of the teacher working with ethnically diverse students, handouts from specialized training in human relations, logos and samples from community-school partnership projects, samples of parental involvement, computer printouts of on-line chats between two classes, and videotapes of a tree planting ceremony at a local nursing home. Students might also include a list of relevant books they've read to demonstrate that their study exceeded class requirements. Such samples illustrate how these students went beyond the standard curriculum, giving more than what was expected. This is a powerful message in any field!

As students complete the formal teacher-training program, a transformation takes place from student portfolio to professional portfolio. Future teaching candidates pull together artifacts that will help them to market their knowledge and skills to prospective school districts. The student portfolio becomes a job search portfolio, addressing the question, "Why should I hire you?"

Portfolios Used for Licensing

Some state education and government agencies have started using portfolios as the basis for employee performance evaluations. This has been spurred by the National Board for Professional Teaching Standards, which has been implementing a rigorous program for national certification of teachers, that includes the portfolio as a major component of the process. Administrator and leadership programs are beginning to ask that their graduates prepare portfolios. It is logical

Case Study—
From Career to Job-Hunting Portfolio

Judith Leng's story is a good example of how a portfolio can evolve from a career decision-making aid into a job-hunting tool. Judith earned her master's degree in teaching English to speakers of other languages (TESOL) at the Monterey Institute of International Studies in 1994. Her intense training program was jam-packed with information, techniques, theories, ideas, tasks, projects, requirements, stipulations, etc. "I was, in a word, totally overwhelmed and had no idea how I was going to make sense of all this newly acquired knowledge about teaching the English language," Judith recalls. She used her portfolio both to sum up her learning experience and to showcase her skills and talents in her job interview:

"In our final college seminar, we were required to include a certain number of items in our portfolio, including samples from our studies, test constructions, lesson plans, curriculum designs . . . the selection was left largely up to us.

"Once I started compiling what I wanted to put in mine, I suddenly realized what an amazing array of things I had accomplished during my time in graduate school. I was absolutely flabbergasted, to tell you the truth. Because suddenly I realized how nicely everything fit together and how each project or paper complemented the other—the theoretical with the practical, the creative with the more strictly academic.

"I had the amazing sensation that, yes, I had learned an incredible amount of information about teaching, and, yes, I could now consider myself quite knowledgeable despite my lack of experience. And that was an immensely gratifying feeling . . . . This document contained the majority of my work, my plans, my successes, my creations . . . my future."

to assume that other professions involving licensure will also consider the portfolio a superior method to the one-dimensional and traditional paper-and-pencil tests that limit what a candidate can demonstrate.

DOCUMENTING PRIOR LEARNING FOR CREDIT

The need for continuous learning is driven by the fact that most of us will change jobs several times in our lifetimes. And for some of these new jobs, we will need retraining, perhaps even another degree or certification. Continuing education takes time—something often in short supply when one is holding down a full-time job. This is when college credit for prior life experiences can be very useful.

Forward-thinking admissions officers and educators in countries like Canada, England, and the United States are designing systems for granting credit based on challenge exams and learning portfolios. These credit-granting options make postsecondary learning more meaningful and more accessible for adults who have acquired significant skills and knowledge from previous experiences (such as travel, independent study, noncollege courses, volunteer activity, and employment). Students who are able to take advantage of the opportunity to gain college credit for life experience save both time and money.

In both Canada and the United States, students returning to school after being in the workforce can now enroll in a course that teaches them how to petition for credits based on prior learning demonstrated through a portfolio. The student begins by summing up his life in an autobiographical chart or essay and then analyzes his personal data for skill content using techniques that resemble those found in chapter 3 on career portfolios. He then pores

When You Don't Have Direct Evidence, Document It with a Letter

Students often choose testimonials or letters to document learning and expertise. These evaluative letters are generally written by former supervisors or mentors. When requesting such a letter, it is helpful if you outline the kind of information that is needed for your portfolio. Have the letter writer:

1. Establish his or her qualifications by listing credentials, years of experience, or current status in the field
2. Describe the relationship with the student
3. Specifically state whether or not the student used the skills being claimed and achieved the stated degree of mastery or proficiency
4. Conclude by evaluating the rank or importance of those skills in the organization

over college catalogs and course syllabi and extracts essential key words and descriptors that summarize prior learning and work. These words are used to guide his construction of a portfolio and later to describe the contents of the portfolio in terms related to course work.

At City University in Bellevue, Washington, for example, students can "reconstruct" up to 45 credits toward a bachelor's degree. In the future, similar options will be extended to graduate-level courses. The final collection is reviewed by faculty or experts in the field to determine the amount of credit to be awarded. Cambrian College in Sudbury, Ontario, also awards credit for lifelong learning outside of school, using exams and portfolio assessments to evaluate students' eligibility.

The Prior-Learning Portfolio Model

A portfolio demonstrating prior learning for credit is not simply a listing of one's work history. You must find ways to verify that college-level learning took place. When describing jobs, begin by recording the traditional information about job title, place, time, supervisor, department, duties, and responsibilities. Expand this later to include information about your training or learning experiences. The final portfolio must include evidence that you studied and acquired new theory or critical-thinking skills.

You can demonstrate this with examples of studies (such as correspondence, book lists, apprenticeship certificates, employee evaluations, travel itineraries, tapes of speeches, certificates for completing seminars and workshops, documents from mentoring programs). Samples of learning may also include licenses, performance or work logs, and evidence of self-study and samples from participation in innovative or unique job experiences such as employee rotation programs or quality circles.

Ultimately, as the portfolio's author, you need to supply a convincing description proving that your knowledge base and skills significantly grew with this additional study. You could illustrate this growth by describing examples of increasing competence, output, quality, or level of responsibility achieved on a job. (As noted earlier, it is helpful to write about these experiences using the vocabulary and terminology associated with the course for which one is seeking credit.)

Sample Outline for Prior-Learning Portfolio

The completed portfolio is submitted to an expert or panel for evaluation and determination of credit. (A summary of various Canadian portfolio programs reported that approximately 90 percent of students who completed a portfolio received some form of credit.) The contents of a typical portfolio submitted for credit are illustrated on the following page. Even if you are not seeking prior-learning credit, this sample will provide you with a good model as you collect information for your portfolio about your ongoing learning.

LEARNING IN A BORDERLESS WORLD

Today's learner is no longer bordered by classrooms. Distance learning is the fastest-growing way to learn today, particularly for the returning student, because it offers good opportunities to fit lifelong learning into busy schedules. As a distance learner, you can take courses in hundreds of subjects—even in creating portfolios—almost anywhere and often on your own schedule, at your own pace.

Distance learning doesn't just mean correspondence courses anymore (although many distance courses do rely on some printed material). It often involves videotapes, audiotapes, TV, and/or computer disks, teleconferencing, Internet research, and interactive student-teacher on-line live forums and e-mail discussions.

Where to Find out About Distance Learning Options

You might want to investigate the resources on the following pages as you examine your learning alternatives:

Virtual College by Pam Dixon (Peterson's, 1996). A quick guide to pursuing courses and degree programs through computer, TV, video, audio, and other

Typical Contents for a Portfolio Demonstrating Prior Learning

I. Title Page
A list with brief descriptions of courses being requested for assessment.

II. Introductory Material
This front material, which can be in the form of a letter, memo, or narrative text, sums up why you believe you are eligible for credit for prior learning experiences.

III. Table of Contents

IV. Chronological Summary or Autobiography
This short essay describes the experiences that have shaped your life, career, and educational goals. List major events, such as jobs; relocations; marriage; parenting; divorce; special achievements in leisure, community, or work life; coaching; travel; health problems; caring for others; supporting oneself with jobs; being laid off; immigration; or learning a new language.

V. Educational Plan and Goals
An outline of your general college education plan with a list of courses already completed for credit, courses being planned for future enrollment, and courses to be evaluated for credit.

VI. List of Skills
Skills may be efficiently described in a résumé format. Describe duties, as well as skills learned on various jobs, programs, and life experiences. (It is helpful to write the skills in terms of learning outcomes that parallel the courses for which you desire credit.)

VII. Appendixes for Documentation (Artifacts)
These include letters, certificates, and samples of work.

---

distance learning media. This book provides important information on distance learning, such as cost of programs, equipment you'll need, credits you can earn, and what it's like being a "virtual" student.

Peterson's Guide to Distance Learning (Peterson's, 1996). An extensive directory of courses, degrees, and certificate programs at colleges and universities with distance learning offerings.

The Internet University: College Courses By Computer by Dan Corrigan (Cape Software Press, 1996). The National Distance Learning Center that can help you locate courses and programs of study on-line. The current listings can be found at http://www.caso.com/iuhome.html. The voice mail number is 502-686-4556 and by Telenet: ndlc.occ.uky.edu.

Portfolios Join the College Career Placement Centers on Campus

If you haven't visited your career planning and placement center on campus before graduation, then you haven't received the full benefit of your education. If you do visit the office, you may very well hear the counselors there advising soon-to-be graduates to include a portfolio in their career planning and job-search arsenals.

In the mid-1990s, the Career Development Center at Michigan State University began asking students to use a portfolio as part of their career planning process. They use the Life Work Portfolio, developed by the National Occupational Information Coordinating Council (Washington, D.C.).

Gail Dunham, assistant director of the center, enthusiastically described these initial efforts in the following way: "Our portfolio program will help MSU students to document and demonstrate their accomplishments in an organized and professional manner. The portfolio not only documents results, but it also documents how the students got those results and what they learned."

Dunham and others point out that the process of articulating skills in a portfolio improves one's ability to communicate skills during an interview. In addition, students enrolled in general academic programs, such as liberal arts, often don't fit neatly into a specific career field. The act of creating a job-search portfolio helps them to frame their educational experiences and orients them toward their future careers.

The Princeton Review Gopher site contains materials related to preparing for standardized tests such as GMAT, GRE, LSAT, and SAT. You can download information from: bloggs. review.com.

The Electronic University Network (EUN) grants degrees, organizes courses of study, and prepares students for earning credits via the College-Level Examination Program (CLEP). EUN is located on America Online at keyword EUN (voice mail: 800-225-3276 toll-free).

Some colleges offer on-line continuing education or extension courses for working people. These classes are often tailored to the specific needs of a given workplace or occupation. Courses range from very technical topics, such as steam plant operations to more general or current issues, such as workforce diversity and sexual harassment.

7

FROM KHAKI TO CIVVIES

Documenting Military Skills and Accomplishments for Civilian Employment Opportunities

▶ Leaving behind the military for civilian employment may be one of life's biggest challenges, comparable to that faced by a person during a midlife crisis, a layoff, or the move into retirement. It totally revamps one's lifestyle. You abandon a known routine and set out for the unknown as you grapple with relocation, changes in finances and benefits, and a whole new set of expectations. A successful transition will depend, in part, on how well you're able to translate military experience into civilian language. A portfolio can help.

Ken Schlueter spent eleven years in Military Intelligence. Today he provides career counseling and job-search assistance to military members (and their families) who are separating from the service.

While in Japan, I conducted a series of mini-interviews with several of my first-time clients. Everyone I talked to believed that a job portfolio would give them a competitive edge. In fact, half of them maintain a binder containing their important military documents or knew of someone who did. One client told me that his buddy kept a "Brag Book." At first, I thought he was talking about a yearbook from Fort Bragg, North Carolina, but it was a binder of his awards and other complimentary documents.

Sonya S. Craft, a job counselor at Fort Bliss JAC, corroborated Schlueter's opinions in her article "The Skills Portfolio: An Answer to the Declining Security Available in Today's Job Market."

The president of a large publishing house observed that today's military alumni possess "a keen sense of mission and purpose; a finely tuned understanding of respect, trust, and the importance of teamwork." He concluded that these qualities make for excellent employees and managers.

He's not alone in his contention: Many employers feel that military people possess valuable experience and character traits. Another chairman and CEO at a large retail chain observed, "I have long believed that Army alumni bring some very special qualities to the private sector. Their dedication—particularly in today's all-volunteer army—is obvious. . . . [They] bring to their jobs and to their lives a wealth of experience that is readily adaptable to the business world."

Employers value the loyalty and dedication found in today's all-volunteer military. Service members learn to value the benefits of hard work. Former service people often present themselves in a respectful, courteous, disciplined, and confident manner. They practice and acquire leadership capabilities during training missions, classes, combat, and competitions. They exit the service with a "can-do" attitude. Sympathetic employers view military people as problem solvers, individuals who know the value of determination and persistence. In addition to the basic skills associated with a specialty or occupation, military personnel often possess collateral capabilities developed during transfers and cross-training. Typical ancillary skills may include managing assets, communicating clearly, maintaining security or self-discipline, understanding the principles of supply economy, developing and following administrative procedures, and budgeting and coordinating personnel and material.

If you are or were in the military, adaptability may be one of your most marketable skills. You live in a world of constant change. One day you show up for work and receive orders to ship out tomorrow. Your mission and location changes throughout military life. Being able to quickly adapt to change fits right into today's lean and mean workplace.

CONNECTING MILITARY JOBS TO CIVILIAN POSITIONS

If you seek civilian work matching your military specialty, then your job-search campaign proceeds forward along a fairly straight line. It gets more interesting when you head off into a full-blown career change. There are many resources available to assist you in choosing a new career and converting military jargon into civilian-friendly terminology. For instance, each branch of the service provides manuals that cross-reference military job titles to civilian titles as outlined in the *Dictionary of Occupational Titles (DOT)*. The Department of Labor has also set up the Transition Assistant Program (TAP) to assist military personnel in making the changeover to civilian life. If you are an officer, you may want to take advantage of the Retiring Officers Association (TROA).

Ken Schlueter reports that regulations for Military Occupational Classification and Structure include codes for both the DOT and the Office of Personnel Management (which is referenced to the Federal Civil Service Classification). For example, the U.S. Army currently uses the following three regulations to provide this kind of information: AR 611-101 "Commissioned Officer Classification System," AR 611-112 "Manual of Warrant Officer Military Occupational Specialties," and AR 611-201 "Enlisted Career Management Fields and Military Occupational Specialties."

As your military exit approaches, you may want to explore various reference books in local libraries or career centers. Working at your own pace in the library, you can browse the lists and references as you brainstorm for new ideas in *The Complete Guide for Occupational Exploration (CGOE)*. This comprehensive work classifies jobs into twelve interest areas and sixty-six general work groups. The *CGOE* shows how to match interests, values, experiences, studies, work experiences, and military occupational specialties to standard job codes found in the *DOT*. All said, forms, references, and regulations will constantly change, but the process of providing assistance to people exiting the service will probably remain intact. It is best to check with career counselors or military staff to find out which types of information are available to you today.

USE YOUR EXISTING MILITARY DOCUMENTS

Regardless of your goal, merely telling the employer that you were responsible for a motor pool is not enough. You'll have to explain how your motor pool experience makes you a competitive, adaptive, dependable employee. As you enter the civilian labor market, you must translate your decorations, awards, ranks, badges, stars, and bars into the common coin of civilian employment.

Fortunately, the service now provides several documents that can assist you in the process of rephrasing successful military experiences in civilian terms. For example, 150 days prior to separation from the service, individuals receive a document entitled "VMET—Verification of Military Education." This is followed by the "DD Form 214—Certificate of Release" or "Discharge From Active Duty" that appears at the time of separation. Schlueter believes that these documents are diamonds in the rough and, when clearly displayed, reveal the many hidden facets of the job seeker's full potential.

The VMET
This is a transcript listing your individual work experience and training history. This form provides information on formal training the individual has undergone plus background about each military occupational specialty that the service member has held. It also lists civilian occupations related to your military work. Associated with each duty and training description is a credit recommendation

from the American Council on Education. A member can also use this transcript to apply for advanced standing at a college or university. The information on the VMET transcript can be very helpful in preparing résumés, negotiating college credits, and applying for federal jobs with specific prerequisites.

The DD214

This provides a "Record of Service" for military members. It contains basic biographical data and verifies rank, branch of service, and military training received. The document lists various job titles and enumerates decorations, badges, and other commendations. Lastly, the form includes a section titled "Special Additional Information," which reveals one's "Character of Service." Schlueter believes that hiring personnel put a great deal of stock in this appraisal because it evaluates overall behavior while on active duty, with the highest rating being an "honorable discharge." Many employers view this characterization as a good predictor of a service member's future behavior on the job. The DD214 also records the actual amount of time spent on active duty, which can increase pay and benefits should the applicant enter federal government employment.

The Personnel Qualifications Records

Most military personnel probably refer to these as the DA 2A (for enlisted soldiers) and DA 2B (for officers). These records are more akin to a résumé than an evaluation report. The printout contains information that the Military Personnel Center deems necessary to store about each service member. The document contains information pertaining to aptitude scores, health profiles, marital status, number of dependents, religion, assignments, and duty titles. Since some of this information is personal and not relevant to a job search, job seekers need to exercise judgment in selecting only those portions that support their career goals.

Additional military documents help round out the applicant's portfolio profile. The Defense Language Proficiency Test (DLPT) verifies foreign language proficiency in over 100 languages. A Security Clearance Notification document testifies to trustworthiness and discipline. Various certificates validate experiences and training in risk-taking areas such as parachuting, high-tech training related to work in air traffic control, proficiency in driving large and complicated vehicles, experience in preparing prescription drugs, etc. Training Certificates will also compare the candidate's achievement to his or her peers. Many times, a person receives commendation for finishing in the top 10 percent of the class.

People leaving the military should also consider including various evaluation documents. Review your Officer Evaluation Report or Non-Commissioned Officer Evaluation Report. In addition to these performance evaluations, there is also an Academic Evaluation Report prepared on any military member undergoing formal schooling. While some of these documents may contain inflated language, you can extract useful ideas and phraseology.

Military life is filled with commendations and awards. While some may be trivial in nature, others must go before the Secretary of Defense or even the Congress for formal approval. The more significant awards require in-depth written justification for the honor. This justification is usually highly laudatory and makes a strong statement about the individual.

Translating into Civilian-ese

Your single most important task in marketing yourself for new employment is to translate your military experience into the language of the civilian labor market. This involves substituting civilian employment lingo for military descriptors in your written and verbal communications and, especially, in résumé and portfolio text. Review the following ten subject headings and try to identify phrases you could use to translate military expertise and experience into civilian-ese.

1. Executes leadership and management responsibilities

   The military trains you to communicate expectations clearly in the form of carefully considered directions and orders. In addition, you are charged with empowering the leadership capabilities of others working under you. As a result, you possess the essential ingredients for managing others because you know how to set examples, motivate others, and guide groups of people. One example may be your team leader experience when you were responsible for analyzing situations, developing options, and accepting responsibility for the outcomes. Another management trait might be your ability to plan and organize. On past ventures or on certain jobs, you may have been responsible for systematically planning, scheduling, and organizing people, time, resources, supplies, and logistics. All of this occurred within the constraints of deadlines, limited budgets, and bureaucracies. You have carried out missions that required constant evaluation of your plans and immediate prioritization of the options at hand.

2. Effectively participates in a diverse and global workforce

   As a result of travel with the military, you may have learned about other cultures, customs, and economic systems. In addition, you may have received training in appreciating cultural diversity, gender equity, and team building. And everyone in the military has practical day-to-day experience working with a broad spectrum of people from various social, educational, economic, and ethnic backgrounds. This prepares you for active participation in increasingly global and diverse workplaces.

3. Demonstrates loyalty, teamwork, cooperative attitudes

   You respect and accept legitimate authority. This includes the ability to work under others, accept supervision, and respond positively to other members of a given crew or team. You know how to follow rules and directives to meet the larger goals of an organization. Loyalty to your leaders and work units has been prized in the past. You know how to work and communicate on a team. You understand what it means to fulfill your duties to a team and remain accountable for your actions.

4. Possesses a strong work ethic and positive work habits

   Various training events, missions, and responsibilities illustrate that you can work under pressure and meet deadlines. You have been schooled and possibly rewarded or recognized for demonstrating integrity, determination, initiative, and problem solving. The military instills a work ethic stressing pride in accomplishment, enthusiasm, and perseverance. You have learned how to work to specified standards of quality or specific outcomes.

5. Understands the link between wellness and productivity

   You appreciate the link between personal wellness and work performance. Your honorable discharge certifies you as a drug-free member of your previous workplace. Your years of service have instilled in you the values and habits that promote physical fitness through conditioning, healthy diet, and a sound outlook on life.

6. Values ethical, confidential, and mature behavior

   Military personnel often achieve a specified level of security clearance. For many employers, an existing clearance will simplify the process of acquiring a civilian or continuing clearance. As noted earlier, this clearance demonstrates trustworthiness, maturity, and a sense of loyalty.

7. Understands the importance of safety consciousness

   You possess the knowledge of specific safety rules, procedures, and attitudes. Previous work records and participation on safety committees, inspections, and problem-solving groups make you a less costly and more safety-conscious worker.

8. Diligently maintains paperwork

   You understand the importance of keeping accurate records and completing paperwork in a timely fashion. In addition, you have learned how your paperwork contributes to your own accountability.

9. Oriented to service and customer needs

   Many military duties and jobs involve providing service to others. This could include working in health, communications, office, financial, recreational, and administrative arenas. Consider situations when you trained others, facilitated meetings or connections, handled correspondence and communiqués, expedited orders and requests.

10. Understands the importance of civic and community contributions

Your very membership in the military proves your value service to others. In addition, you may have contributed to various family- and community-enhancing projects. Perhaps you participated in volunteer youth sports, scouting, family and unit outings, area clean-up days, school mentorships, and school-to-work programs.

Writing Tips

In addition to using the previous phrases (or variations of these) in your portfolio, you'll need to personalize your language by using examples from your particular experiences. Don't just toss the word *leadership* in a caption or phrase—link it to actual personal experiences to make it credible.

Avoid using jargon or stating the obvious. If you merely write "This photo shows the ready-state battalion-level motor pool under my supervision," the reader might be thinking, "So what?" You need to first break down your job description into the component skills that a civilian would understand. Then use the numbers and skill-oriented words to paint the big picture. A more descriptive and more effective caption might read, "It took thorough planning and excellent communication skills to maintain over 100 vehicles in a constant ready state."

Link the Artifact to the Occupation

Once you've found the right words to describe your military experience, use your new civilian-oriented vocabulary to highlight and explain the relevant portfolio documents (such as VMET transcripts, certificates, or medals). To help your prospective employer connect with your artifacts, you'll need to add some descriptive captions to the portfolio.

Placing a combat training picture in your portfolio means nothing unless you write about leadership, preparation, and confidence. If you are going after a sales job, the caption could read, "I'm prepared to aggressively penetrate new markets by combining the can-do attitude and perseverance mastered in my previous career."

Many military people complete advanced degrees while in the service. Take the title page from your thesis and use it as a background sheet. Atop this page, place a picture of a civilian activity or business that relates to your thesis. In your caption, explain how the thesis applies to the particular industry, a specific business practice, or a valued work trait.

Stories You Can Use

The following three fictional stories help illustrate how military artifacts can serve in your portfolio with distinction. These were developed with the help of Ken Schlueter and are based on real service alumni portfolios.

Sergeant Major Holmes

Sergeant Major Holmes is retiring after twenty years of service in the military. He is especially proud of the fact that he was always able to learn his new roles rather quickly and, as a result, became a productive member of the team soon after beginning a new assignment. The military quickly recognized his ability and promoted him to the highest level in the enlisted ranks. To demonstrate this, Holmes has copied a section out of his DA 2A (Personnel Qualifications Record) and used a yellow highlighter to draw attention to the line listing his date of rank and the date he was promoted to Sergeant Major. Beneath the DA 2A form, he wrote a caption for this document that read:

The above highlighted item reflects the date I was promoted to Sergeant Major. I left the military with the highest rank for enlisted personnel.

Holmes went to the base library and obtained a copy of the promotion list that included his name in the *Army Times* newspaper. The accompanying article stated that the average person takes 18.5 years to reach Sergeant Major. In Holmes' case, he was promoted with sixteen years of service. He found a way to create an insert that would hold this article on the same page as the DA 2A. SGM Holmes added the following to his caption:

Due to my ability to learn quickly and to become a productive member of the team in a minimal amount of time, I was promoted to the highest enlisted rank in the military 2½ years earlier than my peer group.

Captain Kendricks

Captain Kendricks was an attorney with the Judge Advocate General Corps. He has significant experience as both a prosecutor and a defense lawyer for the U.S. Army. His job objective following military service was to obtain a position as a legal counsel and staff manager for a U.S. congressional representative, senator, or congressional committee. In his portfolio, Captain Kendricks included a copy of his transcripts from law school, certificates of good standing with the bar association, and a writing sample from an important precedent-setting case. In addition, Captain Kendricks added a selection from his Officer Evaluation Reports describing the time he served on active duty with the military. Captain Kendricks put all of these documents into a single section about military service. The introduction to his evaluations reads:

These reports summarize a successful career in the military. Over this period of time, I was consistently recommended for promotion ahead of my peers. Several reports mention my successful leadership style. This was noted not only by my immediate rater but also by my senior rater. I believe this demonstrates my potential for being a successful manager in the civilian workforce.

Sergeant Sara Reed

Sergeant Sara Reed worked in an Army transportation unit. She was licensed by the military to drive everything from forklifts up to 18-wheelers. She wanted to get a job with an over-the-road trucking company following her stint in the military. During her military service, Reed drove over 125,000 miles without an accident. As a result of her outstanding driving record, Sergeant Reed was awarded a Driver's Badge with a citation describing her feat. During the awards ceremony, the unit photographer took a picture of her receiving the badge from the battalion commander.

Reed felt that this accomplishment would impress her future employer. She put in several hours designing an aesthetically pleasing design that integrated on a single page her driving record, photo, and award. In her caption she wrote:

This photograph and citation document my recognition for driving over 125,000 miles without a single accident or safety violation. This accomplishment is the result my defensive driving abilities, strict adherence to the rules of the road, and my philosophy of safety first. I safely delivered the goods on time!

PUT YOURSELF INTO TRANSITION TRAINING

The portfolio can help you at the front end of a career change when you need to assess your interests, talents, and possibilities. It comes back into play in the final stretch when you use it to present your accomplishments at an interview. If you are facing a multitude of issues upon leaving the military, such as counseling, education, employment, finances, and relocation, you should also consult with career experts and talk with people who have made successful transitions. Harry Drier's book *Out of Uniform: Guide to Military Transition to Civilian Employment* also provides an excellent listing of the various resources available. Drier sums up the challenge with the following advice:

There are three individuals who usually can impede your successful employment transition: yourself, yourself, and yourself. You need to put yourself into transition training like any athlete does so you are prepared and confident to present your winning side.

PART II

Performing Portfolio Alchemy

From about 100 A.D. up through the Middle Ages, alchemists in the Grecian, Islamic, and Chinese civilizations studied metallurgy in an attempt to transmute base metals into gold. In the twentieth century, scholars view the alchemists' pursuit of a perfect metal as an allegory for a larger spiritual quest in life.

In this book alchemy is about the magic of transforming everyday objects like artifacts into an entity with new properties that transcend its origin. We're now at that point where you'll create some alchemy of your own by transmiting your collection of everyday objects into career gold, so to speak. Part II sets forth the steps for doing this.

JUST THE ARTIFACTS

Creative Approaches to Collecting and Crafting Artifacts

▶ Part I was designed to fill your mind with notions of what you'd like to archive. I'm guessing that as you read the chapters and the appendixes, you might have said, "Oh, I wish I had kept my childhood . . ." or "I wonder if I still have that letter my boss wrote when I. . . ." Sometimes, we live through important events and there is simply no trace, no artifact, left behind. After studying under an important leader in your field, do you find you lack evidence of this interaction? You spent several months planning a groundbreaking party for the new building headquarters, and the only thing you retrieved was the party napkin with a great quote you jotted down.

Not to worry. Get creative!

Crafting artifacts is patterned after the inventive techniques used in the résumé-writing business. Résumé professionals describe what their clients actually do rather than relying on bland job descriptions. For instance, suppose your job changed to the point where you are actually running the office and supervising staff, but you still retained the old title of "secretary" on the organizational chart. A professional résumé writer would upgrade the work title to "office coordinator" or "office manager" in order to give a more complete picture of what you actually do. By fine-tuning the language, your résumé more accurately reflects the responsibilities attached to your job title(s) and portrays you in richer detail. A similarly creative method needs to be taken with artifacts.

Creative approaches often take shape in one of three forms.

1—TELLING THE STORY BEHIND A COMMONPLACE ARTIFACT

In this approach, you take a fairly nondescript item and explain its significance, as Isabel Nye did with her flower vase. Her story demonstrates how the principle of embellishment turns everyday articles into powerful portfolio elements. Isabel worked as an instructional assistant in a high school. At the end of the year, the faculty recognized her for her unbounded enthusiasm and coordination of several social gatherings. Her potluck affairs drew people out of their isolating classrooms and into the gaily decorated lunchroom. The Cinco de Mayo lunch was the topper—with homemade empanadas and Latin music. The ordinarily sterile lunchroom sprouted a festival of friendship amidst the delectable aromas of Spanish food. At the end of the year, Isabel was honored with a vase that everyone pitched in to buy.

She put the vase on a shelf and occasionally tells its story to curious guests. And while the award might be briefly mentioned in a résumé, it is probably more impressive to include a picture of the vase in a professional portfolio, accompanied by a caption that might read:

> *I believe that the bonds of friendship we form at work become the foundation for teamwork and cooperation. The various social events that I organize at work help to foster a sense of community and mutual support. During the 1995 employee recognition ceremony, I received this vase for my efforts.*

Even If You Have Limited Experience

If you're a first-time job hunter, you might worry that you have no real work experience to draw upon, not even a vase. You're wrong! Review your previous training and preparation. Brand-new teachers can include photos about student teaching or internships or the memo thanking them for chaperoning that wild spring dance. If you are seeking a management or leadership position, include the award you received for directing the campus service project. If one of your professors read your paper out loud in a seminar, include it as an example of your expertise or communication skills.

If your formal work experience is limited, look at the artifacts related to hobbies and volunteer work. For instance, the skills and knowledge needed for editing and producing the newsletter for your local hospice facility can be transferred to any workplace that uses desktop publishing. As you edit the newsletter you probably use critical thinking abilities, sensitivity, and sound judgment. Such assets can be brought out in your portfolio's introduction and captions or revealed in the letters of reference or newspaper articles you include in it.

2—CRAFTING A SYMBOLIC ARTIFACT

You may want to use an artificial object to symbolize a complex experience or represent an artifact that doesn't exist. My wife received an incredible bouquet of flowers one year from a family grateful for her untiring assistance. She had gone out of her way to monitor the student's work, make weekly phone calls, and serve as a go-between in several key meetings. The flowers have since faded, but Judy could purchase an artificial rose and place it in the center of her portfolio page, describing the quality of work it represents and the subsequent response and recognition she received.

Create List, Log, or Visual Display

When you don't have an "official document" to work with, you can represent a significant effort using a list, log, chart, graph, or other visual display of data. For example, you can assemble a log sheet showing the hours of overtime you put in on an important project, create a list of the committees you served on, compile the dates and names of conferences and seminars attended, summarize the books you've read to keep abreast of current trends, list the names and backgrounds of leaders under whom you studied. If you enjoy using computers or making visual aids, construct a graph to visually display the increasing volume of daily phone calls, e-mail, or voice messages requiring your attention. Include a brief report listing the clients processed, cases closed, transactions completed, or volume of sales achieved.

Summarize with a Case Study, Report, or Story

Alternately, you can make an artifact by summarizing a process. For instance, you can create a flowchart or bulleted report summarizing the steps in a complex project like a media campaign, marketing strategy, or procedure for reducing costs. Suppose your project involved reducing turnover of new accounts for an on-line service. This is sometimes called *churn*. Your list of strategic moves might look like the following:

Strategy for Reducing Churn

- Gathered input from on-line subscribers
  internal: gathered names for people who recently quit the service
  external: gathered industry-wide reports on "churn rates"
  on-line: conducted a survey similar to a focus group but in an on-line
    discussion group

- Compared our churn rate and reasons for quitting with other companies

- Developed a "beginner's" service that addresses the specific needs of people who don't stay on-line for very long

- Modified system interface to make it more user-friendly

- Tested new service and interface with control group

- Evaluated results

- Completed an expanded proposal based on this study

In addition, you can write a case study illustrating how you organized and executed a fairly complex task or project. Suppose it is important to show that you are future-oriented, possess an entrepreneurial spirit, practice peer-mediation for conflict resolution, or utilize employee empowerment to improve productivity. The best stories don't tell everything; rather, they highlight the main points. Begin by making a list of what you did and the outcomes, then turn the list into a short story or case study illustrating your methods. To make the story interesting, be sure to include the problems or risks you faced. Try to keep this story to one page or less.

3—GREATNESS BY ASSOCIATION

The final method illustrates how you can claim greatness by association. Internet and job-search expert Margaret F. Riley cited a colleague's work on her Web page. Her colleague later printed out the page and included it in his portfolio for his next performance evaluation. He used the sample to prove his professional standing among his peers.

Does this sound far fetched? It's not at one Canadian college, which grants credit for prior learning based on portfolios. The student manual encourages students to record conversations with experts and turn in the written transcript as evidence of learning.

Like the résumé writer, you can improve upon the basic information so long as you do it in an ethical fashion and claim no more than is fair.

Did you work diligently behind the scenes while others grabbed headlines? Were you the reliable coworker who kept the operations going while the media distracted your colleagues? Then clip a headline from the paper and store it as a symbol of your coolheadedness. Have you made a special effort to keep current in your field? Then you can create a collage out of the mastheads from the journals you conscientiously read. What about that new book that totally encapsulates your view on the emerging trends shaping your occupation? Remove the book's dust cover and archive it. In the caption, explain how you applied the book's principles to improve performance at work.

Suppose you worked for a high-pressured, 50 plus-hour-a-week company known as a leader in its field. You could assemble a collage to demonstrate your level of commitment and place it over a background testifying to the reputation of your company. Begin by "wallpapering" the document with descriptive copy and photos of the company taken from brochures, annual reports, or information found in the library or on-line. Over that, at the top center, place a picture or sample from a project that you worked on that required a great commitment, perhaps hours and hours of overtime. You may want to add a typical time slip or other data summary showing the amount of time you put into the project. In this fashion, you show the part you played in helping to maintain the firm's excellent reputation. Below it place a short caption. The key is to keep the collage simple and easy to read. You may want a professional graphic designer to assist in the creation of this page. They can use computer scanners, cameras, and other tools to give it a professional look.

The seasoned portfolio author learns to keep an eye out for the treasures and trophies that float past in a spontaneous fashion. To avoid losing these valuable items, chant the portfolio mantra: Store . . . archive . . . collect.

9

CONTENT AND CAPTIONS

Selecting the Contents and Writing Supporting Text

▶ At some point, you'll stop archiving and cataloging and begin thinking about your final portfolio. One critical question must be answered before you begin this process: Who will be viewing your portfolio? If it will be people who know you and your work, then you'll have quite a bit of latitude in choosing what goes into it. But if you are showing the finished product to strangers, then you need to think in terms of a more formal and well-organized display. After all, these strangers are potential customers for your talents, time, and resources.

A portfolio clearly tailored to your audience members can speak to them at various levels. Some samples should possess an emotional impact or quality, while others must speak from a cerebral or analytical viewpoint. A few samples need to have numbers, facts, statistics, or any data that quantifies your efforts at work. A few need to speak to intangible qualities like humor, persistence, or flexibility.

In other words, you must gear your portfolio to your audience. You cannot use the same portfolio for a bank and a student loan, for a job interview and an employee evaluation. While you may draw all your artifacts from the same career portfolio, the items have to be organized and presented differently.

For example, Alan's career portfolio includes samples of his work in the human resource field, where he freelanced as an executive-level manager and consulted for various businesses. Over the years, Alan has constructed different portfolios based on different themes: total quality management, managing change-agents, and employee communication skills. When visiting or interviewing with people, he includes those samples that best pertain to his "customers'" needs.

Keep an Ethical Portfolio

When you're including work-related artifacts, respect your company or employer and make sure you are not compromising any secrets or sensitive materials. Remember, you can always summarize your efforts rather than give detailed descriptions, including just a sample rather than an entire document and being sure to delete names or specifications from writings. When in doubt, simply ask permission before including a confidential or sensitive work sample.

THINKING LIKE YOUR CUSTOMER

In her book *The Advertising Portfolio, Creating an Effective Presentation of Your Work*, Ann Marie Barry advises her readers to do a little homework before assembling their portfolios. She urges advertising people to find out as much as they can about a prospective company and then tailor their sample-advertisements portfolio to the needs of the employer in general and the creative director in particular. In other words, match the contents of the portfolio to the interests and needs of the person or people making the hiring decision. Barry even suggests creating speculative ads related to products the company has represented in the past. Doing this demonstrates knowledge of the agency's past work and the ability to meet its needs and match its style. (This concept of speculative ads is similar to the process of creating artifacts, discussed in chapter 8. If you want to get additional ideas from Barry, read the chapter in her book called "Creative Approaches to Collecting or Crafting Artifacts.")

If you design the portfolio for a specific employer, then you'll want to pick samples that match the requirements or needs of the prospective position. In the past, it was enough to include transcripts, examples of technical skills, references, résumés, and evaluations. But today you may need to go further in demonstrating your abilities. You'll also want to focus on certain personal qualities or temperaments such as enthusiasm and flexibility. You need to prove that you think more like an entrepreneur or business partner than an employee. Can you find samples from your previous work that show how you increased profitability, reduced costs, or, in the case of public-service work, saved public funds or resources? Do you have examples of how you've kept up with the latest trends in management, computer skills, or communications?

If you are unsure what is appropriate in your line of work, then ask around, conduct your own survey, visit your reference librarian. You can gather information by reading professional journals, attending conferences, talking with people working in your profession, both informally and in informational interviews. There is also the digital option: Log on to electronic bulletin boards and forums where current issues in your field are being discussed. Research potential employers by visiting their home pages on the Internet (for more on doing research on the Internet, see chapter 13).

Your goal is to show how your talents and experiences can be put to use in meeting the organization's goals. It is important to select portfolio artifacts that illustrate your ability to deliver solutions or bring value-added experience to the people examining your portfolio.

HOW MANY SAMPLES SHOULD YOU INCLUDE?

Sue Sherbert helps college graduates at the University of Northern Iowa turn their student portfolios into professional job-search tools. Often students walk into her office with a portfolio too large to carry and announce they are ready for job interviews. "I couldn't help but wonder if the employer would think the applicant brought the family album!" she humorously remarked when telling me that story. "I knew I had to address the question of appropriateness."

How extensive should your portfolio be? For education or school portfolios, the answer is easy—the institutions themselves often prescribe what needs to be included. An applicant may be asked to include specific information in the portfolio's introduction, the types of work samples, and to follow special directions for format and presentation. But in the larger job market, the answer is not so clear.

In a professional portfolio, what you include is just as important as what you leave out. It is far better to put only five or so outstanding examples in a portfolio than to load it with many more mediocre ones. For example, five work samples that clearly match the requirements of the job for which you're applying are superior to ten somewhat redundant letters of reference, where only a few of the talents mentioned may directly apply to the position. Place your most impressive items at the front and end of the sequence when possible.

In sum, only include your best. This is especially true of written materials. Scrupulously review and eliminate any writing that contains errors. Also, don't include anything that could be offensive in terms of politics, religion, lifestyle, or the like. Reconsider any report, editorial, or posters you completed on a hot political or social issue unless you are certain that your audience completely agrees with both your content and style. Finally, you need not include bulky items such as large reports, detailed curriculums, and databases. Simply refer to these items and include representative samples, a synopsis, or a table of contents.

You can always take more to an interview or presentation than you plan to show. Generally, don't expect people to absorb more than six to ten samples. Afterwards, the decision makers may want to keep your entire portfolio as they pore over the paperwork of the final candidates.

In general, keep your portfolio as brief as possible. There are exceptions to this rule, however. When applying for a business loan, your business portfolio should approximate the contents of a business plan. A portfolio designed for potential customers of your products or services should show versatility and diversity and, therefore, may exceed twenty items.

The next exercise will help you think about your audience, the kinds of information that could meet their needs, and the length of the final portfolio.

Ask the Rights Questions

Think of the portfolio presentation and interview as a dialogue revolving around two essential questions facing all the participants: "How can this person help me?" and "What assistance, resources, information, or support does this person need from me?" Finally, to put yourself in a framework for selecting specific artifacts, begin thinking of yourself as a supplier and the employer as a customer. Viewed in this way, you progress to the final question: "What are my assets; what do I have to sell?"

Your years of experience, reputation, and contacts are all invaluable resources. If you were a salesperson, you could take your Rolodex of customers to the interview and mention it as one of your assets. Specialty skills picked up as a hobby or on the job are also assets. These might include a foreign language, repair work, public-speaking experiences in a group like Toastmasters International, and evaluation skills used as a volunteer member on an advisory board.

▶ EXERCISE #11
Analyzing Your Audience

Use the three questions mentioned above to help focus on the needs of your audience rather than your own needs. This is essential because when you look at the audience's needs first, you increase your chances of closing the sale or getting the offer. With a sense of your audience firmly in place, follow the steps below to develop an audience analysis for your portfolio. (This analysis will also work in the design of your résumé.)

1. Sum up your "market research" in the column on the left. If you only have a general sense of what things customers or employers are looking for, write them down and then ask around, conduct the necessary research interviews, or do more reading to zero in on their needs.

2. When you think you have a good sense of the audience's needs, make an inventory of your assets, and try to develop a match. You might find Appendices C and D near the back of this book helpful in describing your skills.

Market Research Ledger	
Audience Needs: What They Want (List skills, duties, qualities)	**Assets:** What I Have (List artifacts to describe assets)
Examples: • Leadership • Experience managing projects • Ability to gather attention on the Internet • Knowledge of foreign markets	Examples: • Service club award • Time line for a large project • Web page I designed • List of foreign languages and international organizations you belong to

3. Describe what your audience members might be like—their personalities, appearance, mannerisms. Then speculate about the kinds of questions they might ask. (Visualizing your audience in this fashion is a technique used in writing workshops. Authors of nonfiction works are often advised to make a profile detailing their readers. They then place this description near the keyboard as they compose their work. Whenever the writing slows down or a passage becomes problematic, the writer stops and asks, "Will my readers understand this? What do my readers want?" Audience always comes first!)

In the end, you need to be able to describe the product (in the case of your portfolio—you) and its benefits to the customer's or employer's satisfaction. This does not mean lying about the product or deceiving yourself about the job. If it isn't a match, the proposition will ultimately lead to a "no sale."

With the final artifacts selected, consider next how each item could be described with captions and summaries.

CREATING CAPTIONS AND SUPPORTING TEXT

Exhibits do not speak for themselves. You must connect the dots for the viewer—connect the artifacts with the audience's interests. If you want employment, then articulate, for instance, how the photo of your volunteer experience building low-income housing prepares you to meet the challenges of working in a real estate firm. A caption connecting the work sample to an audience of realtors could sound like this:

In 1995, I worked for Habitat for Humanity. I learned how homes are put together, and I currently use this knowledge to describe quality construction to my real estate clients. I also believe that customers who are about to make an investment in our community respect me more because they appreciate my investment of time in the same community.

▶ # EXERCISE #12
Writing Captions

A picture of a team or a ribbon from an ice-skating competition shows your favorite sport, but it doesn't tell the whole story. What did it take to get the ribbon? How many hours were spent, and what sacrifices were made? Did the group as a whole set a goal or take a pledge? From an employment perspective, how would the lessons about teamwork apply to the workplace? What did you have to learn in order to function more effectively on a team with many different personalities?

This exercise introduces the task of writing captions. You generally have a limited amount of space next to your artifact for a caption but in this exercise, don't limit yourself to any length. You can always extract the best lines later.

1. Educators often ask their students to write something about each item exhibited in their portfolios. They ask their students to answer the following:

- What is being shown?

- How did you accomplish the task or how did you use your skills?

- Why is this included; why is it important?

   Learning how to articulate the *what, how,* and *why* of an artifact is the first step in developing supporting text or captions. Portfolio instructors usually prompt their students with questions such as those in the following list. The phrase in parentheses that accompanies each question shows a sample skill or employment ability related to the question. This serves to remind the writer that each artifact comes embedded with evidence of a skill. Pick one of your favorite artifacts and then answer each question below as it pertains to the experience represented by that sample:

- How did you apply what you know? What additional learning took place? (self-directed learning)

- How did you communicate ideas in this experience? Was it through a committee, computer, performance, public speaking, e-mail, etc.? (communication)

- Was the length of time involved significant? (endurance, persistence)

- What challenges did you face and how did you meet them? (problem solving)

- Were you given (or did you assume) more responsibilities? Why? (responsibility, leadership)

- Were you promoted or given a raise? Why? (recognition of effort, leadership)

- What changes did you have to make as you went along? What compromises? (flexibility)

- What changes were made in policy or procedure due to your input? (contribution, teamwork)

- What kinds of information had to be gathered or presented? (organization, research)

- What will you miss about the place? (reputation, team spirit, mission, vision)

- Who benefited the most from your presence? Describe why or how. What impact did you have? How do you know you did a good job? (accomplishment or outcomes)

- Who was involved? Who will miss you and why? (contribution)

2. Next, write captions for two more artifacts addressing the *what, how,* and *why* to tell the story behind the artifact. In this fashion, train yourself to ask questions like those above prior to writing captions.

Add Quantifiable or Numerical Data

Some people are persuaded by messages with emotional content, and others want just the hard facts. To make sure that you reach both types of audiences, add factual-sounding phrases or quantifiable descriptors to some of your captions. This might include numbers or phrases indicating a degree of change as in "sales increased by 65 percent."

Quantities can be found in the number of hours put into a project or improvements that resulted in quantifiable increases in positive factors such as profits, employee satisfaction, phone requests, and output. Also, look for numbers or phrases indicating a decrease in negative or costly events including turnover, long-distance calls, complaints, and injuries. You can also describe what was done in terms of size or numbers of people involved. How many participated, how large was the convoy, what size was the garden, and how large was the display? The next two examples show how numbers and quantitative phrases can add punch to a caption.

The above photo shows our product display at a national convention. The display was 25 feet by 12 feet, lit by thirty-five lights, and attracted 1,000 more customers than the booth next to it.

This table of contents is from my report Low-Cost Alternatives for Tracking Pharmaceutical Products. This report summarizes data from 1,500 respondents. The results clearly demonstrate that front-end scanner systems improve profit margins by 25 percent. This report was later used by our executive council and referred to in numerous professional manuals.

If you lack hard numbers, you can use language that describes the direction or magnitude of improvements made at work (i.e., decreased return rate). Phrases such as *most, more, less,* and *least* connote the degree of change, whereas words like *increase* or *decrease* spell out the direction. You can give your wording a quantifiable ring with something like the following:

After the training, I designed a no-reject customer-service plan, which resulted in a dramatic decline in the number of complaints filed.

The team-building retreat I planned and led resulted in an increased sense of morale and cooperation in all who attended.

After writing a caption, let it sit. Then review it with an eye for adding numbers or descriptive phrases that quantify changes, effectiveness, or outcomes.

10

ORGANIZATION

Methods for Grouping and Sequencing: Chronological, Functional, Thematic, Specialized

▶ With your audience firmly in mind, artifacts selected, and captions completed, it's time to think about organizing the contents of your professional portfolio. Generally, each portfolio page should contain three items: an artifact, a caption, and a title. When similar experiences or talents are grouped together in sections or mini-chapters, your portfolio reflects a thoughtful order and clear story line.

There are two main ways to organize a résumé: chronologically and by function. Both can be used with portfolios, and so can a third style, the thematic approach, where content is organized by major themes.

If most of your experience is in the same field and you can demonstrate increasing growth and accomplishment, then it's simply a matter of organizing your career history by dates, using the chronological method. However, a pure time-line approach is not very readable. Therefore, experiences are generally grouped into categories first and then in chronological order within these categories. Each category represents a block of similar kinds of experiences and is set off by a title or heading. Categories are typically grouped in three to five of the following areas:

- Work experience
- Education
- Awards and certificates
- Special skills
- Personal accomplishments or background

However, in today's fluid world of work, most people's careers are no longer effectively described in a linear, chronological listing. Many people (and the numbers are growing) experience interruptions in their work, training, and education. For instance, if you're working in the travel business, your career may occasionally be stalled by downturns in the industry. During periods of unemployment, you might pursue in-between jobs working for a shipping line, chamber of commerce, or travel bureau.

Most people with either limited or varied work experience find that they can tell a better career story when they group their experiences by common function rather than by date, in what is generally known as the functional résumé. In such an organization, the headings reflect areas of expertise or common themes. Examples vary as much as one's work history.

Consider Nina, a travel agent who has periodically left the business during slow times to take up temporary work in her local public library. Nina has also done telemarketing out of her home and filled in as a substitute night manager for various local store owners (who were also her previous travel customers). She may choose to group her experiences under the following headings:

- Travel experiences
- Sales and marketing
- Customer service (library)
- Management experiences

ADAPTING RÉSUMÉ WRITING STRATEGIES

Most people opt for a hybrid organization of their résumé, combining the best of both the chronological and functional types. They group their experiences by categories that reflect their skills. When grouping your experiences under various titles or headings, you must carefully evaluate and examine your organizational scheme against one question: Do the headings support your career objective or goal listed at the top of your résumé? Specific experiences are then listed by chronology or importance within each category. At the end of the résumé, you may place a brief chronological summary of work or experiences.

This history should account for periods of unemployment by listing activities that involved, for instance, self-study, going back to school to learn a new occupation, volunteer work, or caring for an ill family member. It is pointless to simply state you were unemployed. In Nina's case, she needed to account for the year she took off to take care of her mother. During that time, she got hooked on meeting people on-line; she called it her digital lifeline to the world.

When Nina later enrolled in a telecommunications program, she realized that she enjoyed the social aspects of cyberspace more than the technical ones.

After her mother died, she wanted to take some time off for herself. She decided to go back to work on a part-time basis and returned to the travel industry as a temporary worker. Eventually she became engaged full-time in the business. She translated all of these experiences into the vocabulary of work and presented her history as shown here:

Work and Experience Summary	
1982–1988	Well Wishers' Travel Group
1988–1989	Home Health-Care Provider (self-employed)
1990–1991	Student (engaged in formal study and self-study of telecommunications)
1992–1994	Management Support Staff
1990–Present	Travel Agent (freelance work)

Portfolios can be organized using a similar approach, but the most powerful portfolios are ones in which the author develops a personalized set of categories rather than the standard groupings of work, education, and professional organizations. Creating a meaningful sequence or categorical scheme takes some thought on your part. You've got to analyze your skills and interests and think deeply about the passions, styles, and themes reflected in your line of work.

If you completed the exercises in chapter 3, then you are ready to start thinking about the four general ways of organizing your portfolio's content. Pick one that seems easiest and try it first. Then try an alternate method of organization so that you can make a comparison. Remember, just as with résumés, hybrid styles are possible.

THE CHRONOLOGICAL PORTFOLIO

This is the simplest portfolio to make. It is well-suited for scrapbooks, photo albums, and other forms of the personal portfolio. A time-based or chronological sequence can turn an eclectic mix of papers, awards, letters, photos, printouts, and journal entries into a coherent and logical collection. This system works best if there has been constant improvement and growth in your life.

A sample outline for one such portfolio is shown on the following page. It belongs to a student who wants to enter political life as a legislative assistant.

THE FUNCTIONAL PORTFOLIO

A functional portfolio is often the most useful because you can assemble the artifacts around skill sets related to the work you are seeking. But in order to do

Chronological Portfolio Outline

College Life

I. **Early Studies 1997–1998**
   A. Transcripts from Required Courses
   B. Certificates of Appreciation from Service Clubs
   C. Special People Who Shaped My Thinking

II. **Introduction to Campus Politics 1998–1999**
   A. The Campaign for Vice President
   B. Representing Our School at Conferences
   C. Dean's List and GPA Record

III. **Career Goals 1999–2001**
   A. Career Goals
   B. Supporting Letters of Reference
   C. Graduate School Acceptance Letter
   D. Résumé

IV. **Self-Evaluation**
   A. Journal: "News Junky: Eating and Breathing Politics."

this successfully, you need to establish an organizing principle for connecting your many artifacts. Below, you can see that the contents of the chronological outline has been reworked into a functional outline. In this instance, the common features of various artifacts guide the creation of different functional groups. All the material related to evaluation is grouped first, while the material listed under Introduction to Campus Politics in the chronological outline have been regrouped under Public and Professional Service, and a new catagory for Communication Skills is added.

If you find that your skills in a given field come from a potpourri of different experiences or different times, you'll find the functional outline better suited to your needs. This style is also useful when you lack significant or long-term experience, especially when you are changing career fields or just graduating

Functional Portfolio Outline

College Life

I. **Evaluations—GPA, test scores, and narratives**
   A. Entering SAT Scores
   B. Grade Transcripts
   C. Dean's List
   D. Letter of Reference from Student Senate Advisor

II. **Public and Professional Service**
   A. Election Results for Vice President
   B. Samples from Conference Presentations
   C. Community Service Fund-Raising Projects

III. **Communication Skills**
   A. Internet and Desktop Publishing
   B. Recruitment Letters and Direct Mailers
   C. Résumé
   D. Award-Winning Essay: "Apathy or Advancement"

from a program. Use the functional approach when you want to connect various short-term experiences together to show a long-term interest in a given field or skill.

THE THEMATIC PORTFOLIO

A portfolio organized around themes can result in a very evocative product. This way of organizing materials was introduced in Exercise #8: Looking at Work Thematically in chapter 3. You might want to review this exercise prior to choosing themes for different sections of your portfolio. It may be easier to practice thinking about a thematic portfolio for events in your past, rather than for those in your present, because time can often give you fresh perspective.

I once constructed a retrospective fictional high school portfolio using a theme-based approach to illustrate the process in a portfolio workshop for high school teachers. I went back in time, gathering up memorabilia from long-ago days, and developed the table of contents and introduction that you see in Artifact #3.

The title on the front page of my professional portfolio is stated in thematic language. I also include a quote to extend the theme. A sample from the title page and table of contents is shown in Artifact #4. Each sample appears on its own page so that I can select those I want as needed for job interviews, grant proposals, media interviews, and the like.

Notice that the thematic summary in the table of contents in Artifact #4 almost serves as a functional résumé in itself. I only used this complete collection in an interview once because I always felt it was too long. On an earlier occasion, when it was a bit shorter, the person who ultimately had to decide my future work destiny took the complete portfolio home and reviewed everything. He later offered me the job.

ORGANIZATIONAL ALTERNATIVES

In addition to the basic chronological, functional, and thematic portfolio styles, you can invent your own approaches or adapt ideas from other sources.

The Special Report
One of the most intriguing job-search tools around is the special report, a concept developed by career adviser Jack Chapman, author of *How to Make $1000 a Minute Negotiating Your Salaries and Raises*.

Unlike a résumé, which focuses on the job seeker and stresses self-promoting descriptions of talents, Chapman's special report focuses on the interests of the reader—the employer. The special report is a summary illustrating how you

Artifact #3

Thematic High School Portfolio

My Years At Woodside High School
1962–66

My high school career began as a rather inauspicious event . . . . I was a strictly average guy. But by the time I graduated, things had changed markedly. This portfolio highlights some of the most important accomplishments of my high school experience, which included participation in sports, drama, student government, community affairs, and an ever-improving grade point average.

I made this portfolio twenty-eight years after graduating from high school. As I look back now, I realize that there were many lessons that took me twenty-eight years to fully grasp. I guess that's the value of hindsight and reflection.

Table of Contents

Performance Is Everything
- Drama Experiences
- Sports Participation

Learning to Serve Others
- Human Relations Club
- Joining and Then Quitting Student Government
- Appreciation Letter from a Parent and Community Member

Finding Meaning in a Difficult Era
- Organizing a Political Debate by Candidates About Vietnam
- Letter to Editor and Reply

Academic Triumph
- Earning Respect from Those Who Disagree with You

Adversity Becomes Me—Thriving on Challenges
- Freshman Report Card
- Senior Report Card
- Membership in Honor Society

Artifact #4

Thematic Career Portfolio

Samples from a Lifelong Journey of Teaching and Learning

Career Portfolio
Martin Kimeldorf

—1975 to the present—

"The greatest distance we have yet to cover still lies within us."

—Contents—

The Interdisciplinary Life

College Transcripts: Education, Art, Technology
Integrating Art and Learning in Theater
FutureSign Revue—Poetry and Technology
Square Root Blues—Linking Art with Math
Samples from student work in interdisciplinary block program:
    freshman studies

Developing Innovative Programming For Kids

Alternative Education
I Trust You with That Ax (Outdoor Crews)
Peer Tutoring—Early Attempts at Integration
Reviews of my book *Creating Portfolios for Success in School,
    Work, and Life*
Articles and Workshops About Self-Directed Job Hunting Programs
School-To-Work Transition Project Newsletter

Contributing and Being Contributed To

Student Teaching and Classroom Evaluations (1975 and 1993)
American Vocational Association (AVA) Editor (1982)
Teacher of the Year 1985
Tools for Teachers brochure (1987)
Letters of Appreciation from State Department of Education,
    Peers, Parents (1980s and 90s)
Legislative Proposal based on my curriculum (1988)
Imagine,—Cover from state report on youth community service (1990)
Award for best paper—*International Journal of Career Management* (1993)
International Award for best paper—*International Journal of
    Career Management* (1993)

Special Report Sample Outline

Thirty-One Ways Health-Care Providers Can Profit from the Coming Shift from Sick Care to Well Care

I. Introduction
The shift from sickness-and-cure philosophy to wellness-and-prevention philosophy.

II. Body
Thirty-one ways to use this trend to build business for hospitals, HMOs, and other health-care institutions.

III. About the Author
A brief synopsis of the author's background.

believe the profitability of an operation can be enhanced through, for example, savings in time, money, or both. In the report, you expand on five to ten ideas, which can include your own set of personal tips, tricks of the trade, basic principles, or mistakes to be avoided. Each idea is described with fifty to 100 words and ends with a rule or suggestion. As a result, the report contains practical, useful information, and the document positions you as an experienced candidate, using the language of the industry or field in which you are seeking work.

A sample outline for a report is illustrated in the box here.

This type of report is generally reserved for people with experience in the work they are pursuing because the advice must demonstrate expertise and depth. If you are a career changer, you need to use a different approach so that your report is based more on research than firsthand experience (of which you probably have little at this time). This research can be based on material you gather in print and electronic media or through interviews with industry experts. In your report, you summarize information of vital interest to someone in the field.

Again, if you're changing careers, you need to clarify in the introduction that your report is a summary of your investigations and relates to your desire to make a career change. You would be wise to get second and third opinions from people well-versed in the field about the merits of your report before distributing it widely. (You can write to Jack Chapman to get more information about his Special Report; his address can be found in the resource section near the back of this book.)

Adapt Chapman's basic model to your portfolios by highlighting problems you can solve. To begin, identify five to fifteen problems in your field. A person in manufacturing might think about production bottlenecks, inventory irregularities, or quality control issues; a health-care specialist could present methods for reducing costs by changing from treating sickness to preventing it through the promotion of individualized wellness plans. Then, for each problem, list one or more methods for solving it.

For instance, under the heading Five Ways to Promote Wellness, your report could describe in brief narrative form the techniques you recommend for promoting wellness and reducing costs. Samples illustrating how you implemented or planned the five methods could follow the list or be put in a separate appendix at the back. In this fashion, you could include the shorter version (minus the samples) when networking and prospecting for leads. Then you can bring the more complete version to an interview. Your report ends with a brief biography or mini-résumé that lists your major accomplishments in the field.

The Teaching-Portfolio Model

Another alternative organization can be found in Peter Selden's book *The Teaching Portfolio*. While Selden's model is tailored to those people seeking tenure in higher education, the process can easily be adapted to other industries. Because his

> ### An Example of Adapting a Special Report to Portfolios
>
> Reducing Insurance Costs by Increasing Wellness
>
> I. Introduction
>   A. Why the Topic is Important to the Field
>   B. My Experiences in Problem Solving
>   C. Summary or Overview of the Report Contents
>
> II. Five Ways to Promote Wellness
>   A. Recognition Ceremonies and Other Incentives
>   B. Flexible Personnel Policies
>   C. Work-Family Programs
>   D. Education and Outreach Examples
>
> III. Appendix
>   A. Newsletter Articles, Awards, Ceremonies
>   B. Flex-Leave, Telecommuting, Graduated Leaves
>   C. Plans for Patient Wellness Discount System
>   D. Mini-clinic Courses in Wellness
>   E. Samples from Family-Friendly Programs
>   F. Chart Showing Cost Reductions
>
> IV. About the Author
>   A. Short Summary of Your Background or Career Highlights Résumé

approach involves a great deal of peer collaboration, it is also a valuable tool for building a team atmosphere. Part of its success depends on support and involvement with supervisors and mentors or department chairpersons. Selden's approach is well-suited to higher education or situations where a committee reviews an employee's performance using performance documentation.

Selden's key organizational principle centers on the six to eight pages of descriptive material at the front of the portfolio. Professors sum up their teaching using examples or products, including videotapes of teaching, samples of student work, and feedback or observations by others. This very personal document begins with a summary of duties and reflective statements and often ends with goals for improving teaching method. Based on his suggestions, a portfolio could be organized as seen here.

While the Teaching-Portfolio Model serves a somewhat specialized purpose, it shares broad similarities to Chapman's Special Report, which is frontloaded with information and supported by a detailed appendix of samples.

Teaching-Portfolio Model

I. Table of Contents

II. Profiling My Work
   A. Teaching Philosophy
   B. Teaching Responsibilities and Objectives
   C. Strategies Used in Teaching (Exams, Computers)
   D. Syllabi and Course Description

IV. Efforts at Achieving Quality Teaching
   A. Peer and Student Evaluations
   B. Journal Reflections
   C. Summary of Teaching Workshop Participation

V. Goals
   A. Strategies to Try Next
   B. Studies Outlined
   C. Conclusion

IV. Appendix
   A. Reading Lists and Course Description
   B. Student Outcomes (Exams, Test and Survey Scores, Employment Statistics)
   C. Other Commentary (Letters from Alumni, Observations by Colleagues)
   D. Situational Evidence (Videotape of Graduate and Undergraduate Lecture)

Both Selden and Chapman illustrate the many possibilities for adapting the portfolio to your unique situation or goals. In both instances, they have placed most of the descriptive material from captions and section headings at the front. Yet, each model serves a decidedly specific purpose, tailored to different audiences. If you are unsure which approach to use, then I'd suggest beginning with the more conservative chronological, functional, or thematic style.

THE OUTLINING PROCESS

As an outline for your sequence unfolds, it should include both headings and subheadings. Headings can then be placed on section pages that introduce each category of artifacts. Think of these as headings for chapters in your portfolio. I often include a separate cover page for each section or group of artifacts. For instance, one chapter heading might be *Technology*, followed by a summary of the software samples that appear in that section. The samples themselves start off with their own subheading, such as *Computer Technology* or *Internet Technologies*. In this manner, I bring a sense of unity to the contents. Eventually, I reuse the outline in the front matter, which usually includes an introduction, table of contents, and sometimes acknowledgments or goal statements. (These elements are further described in chapter 11.)

To rev up your mind for this kind of analysis, it will be useful to review the skill factoring exercises in chapter 3, Exercise #10: Analyzing Portfolio Artifacts Using Occupational Codes (DPT), and also Appendix C: Skill Words. Skill factoring helps you to evaluate the skills or functions that lie behind the experience. Out of this, you can then find the common skills or functions that tie different experiences together and provide you with your headings and subheadings.

I like to begin this part of my portfolio work by physically placing my artifacts in piles. It is important that you not worry about what each pile is called at first because they will constantly shift until you arrive at a suitable system. Perhaps in the beginning, you'll sort artifacts by the system of data, people, and things as illustrated in Appendix C. Next, look for new, unnamed piles that can be formed.

Say, for instance, your samples related to bird watching seem to come closest to the *Things* pile. But on closer examination, you notice that everything else in that pile is about yards, equipment, tools, and landscaping. You move the information about bird watching to the *Data* pile because bird watching requires the ability to record and organize data about sightings. And yet, deep down, you know this pile is not quite right. Finally, you remove the bird-watching samples and place them in a new pile now labeled *Wildlife*. Keep things fluid until you find the connections that make sense to you. It is also

Portfolios with Prescribed Criteria or Outlines

On occasion you may be asked to submit a portfolio to very specific specifications; its content and sequence have been predetermined by external criteria.

For instance, a college granting credit for learning experiences that are demonstrated in a portfolio will often dictate a particular format and arrangement. The form helps to standardize portfolios, which, in turn, eases the task of evaluation by administrators and experts. Standardized portfolios can more easily be measured against standard course descriptions and credit requirements.

A business loan application might be best done by including exhibits related to proof of your financial stability (credit histories), your expertise in the field (degrees, articles, awards), and market demand for your product or service (articles, studies, receipts). You'll want to demonstrate profitability for your ideas, thus increasing the chances of paying off the loan in a timely manner.

Other situations may not require specific items, but there may still be a general pattern to follow. Portfolios for an art show or other similar exhibit often include samples of art work, education, and a biography or statement of philosophy. A scholarship committee might ask that all applicants include several items from a prescribed list of choices, such as writing samples, community service, leadership, self-study, self-discipline or persistence, and academic transcripts.

helpful to get feedback from others; they might give you a whole new perspective on organization.

Finally, review the needs and expectations of your audience. (See Exercise #11: Analyzing Your Audience, found in chapter 9.) Keeping in mind the samples you have and the samples that those reviewing your portfolio will want to see, develop a list of names or labels describing your existing groups of artifacts. In this manner, you'll probably discover new or additional categories more finely tailored to the needs of your audience. Remember, portfolio organization may very well change with each new potential employer, customer, or review board you see.

11

ADDING THE DESIGNER'S TOUCH

General Design Principles and Construction Tips; Developing Front Matter and Closing

▶ In 1982, I finished my first major book on job searching, which I composed using early desktop publishing software. As I think back to that first laser-printed book, an embarrassing grin appears on my face. I used every technique in every menu that the software offered. Anything of note was either put in bold or italic or underline. I used main headers, subheaders, sub-subheaders, and varying inserts, boxes, and columns. The publisher referred to it as the circus-poster book. He was right.

Don't make my mistake: don't produce a circus-poster portfolio. A portfolio is a visually complex piece of work because each page varies according to the artifact, and you need to search for a way to unify the presentation, not complicate it with unnecessary design embellishments. What follows are some general rules for maximizing the visual appeal of your final portfolio, without giving it a circus look.

Several of the design rules here are borrowed from those in desktop publishing and résumé writing. If you wish to learn more, I have listed my favorite books in the Resources section near the back of this book. New books and magazines come out all the time that can help improve your appreciation and awareness of good design.

I find that input from professional designers can be invaluable. My first foray into design literacy came in the form of a workshop about desktop publishing for newsletters. Seeing actual examples of good and bad design in juxtaposition and learning about new trends where headlines and titles are set flush left rather than centered was well worth the cost of admittance. You may also find it worthwhile to consult with a professional graphic artist and designer to critique your first portfolio layout.

USE CONSISTENT PLACEMENT

A unified look to your collection results from placing text and objects in consistent positions on each page. Use at least a 1-inch margin of white space on each page, with an extra ¼-inch on the left side of the page to accommodate the binding. Then reserve the first 1 to 2 inches at the top for a title or heading. When you place captions, be consistent—put them in the same place on each page. You could put a caption right next to the object, especially when there is more than one object per page. I generally tend to put a single artifact on each page with my caption placed in the same 2-inch zone located at the bottom. Thus, as one turns the page, the eye always knows where to look for the title and supporting caption information.

Such consistency helps unify the portfolio's look, even though the contents of a page may vary from a handwritten letter to a photo or a computer chart printout. You can also place objects of varying size in the same relative position if you use a grid or template. Make this grid on tracing paper or on a desktop publishing master sheet and then overlay it on the blank page so that you have a consistent set of spaces for titles, captions, and artifacts. However, don't use a grid that divides the page down the middle. The result is a static, perfectly

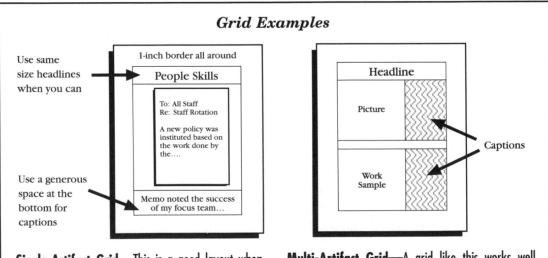

Grid Examples

Use same size headlines when you can

1-inch border all around

People Skills

To: All Staff
Re: Staff Rotation

A new policy was instituted based on the work done by the....

Use a generous space at the bottom for captions

Memo noted the success of my focus team...

Headline

Picture

Work Sample

Captions

Single-Artifact Grid—This is a good layout when you have one artifact per page.

Multi-Artifact Grid—A grid like this works well when you have more than one artifact on a page.

Note: None of the thin guide lines are printed. Try to minimize the number of grids and use them consistently.

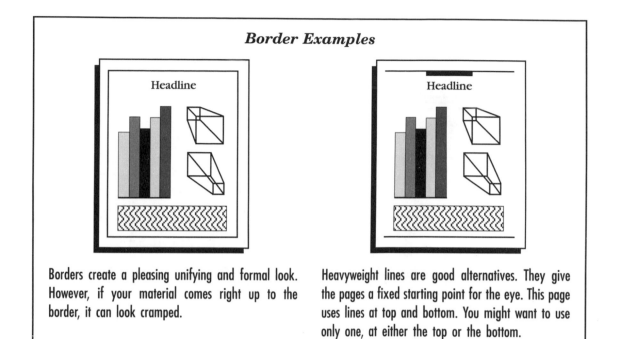

Border Examples

Headline

Headline

Borders create a pleasing unifying and formal look. However, if your material comes right up to the border, it can look cramped.

Heavyweight lines are good alternatives. They give the pages a fixed starting point for the eye. This page uses lines at top and bottom. You might want to use only one, at either the top or the bottom.

balanced layout that stops the eye from examining the rest of the page. Instead, divide the page into two or more unequal zones.

The samples on the previous page use a simple template on each page with the largest zone reserved for the artifact and smaller zones or regions holding titles and caption text blocks.

The more complex your subject or visual element, the simpler your grid should be. If you need to use blueprints, technical or detailed drawings, schematics, or charts, then keep the rest of the page uncluttered by using a simple headline that incorporates the caption.

Also remember that borders and captions need to be used in a consistent manner. These visual guides should play a minimal role—many people opt not to use them at all. There are many options for these design elements and a few are illustrated above and on the following page.

USE CONSISTENT TYPOGRAPHY

You can further unify the look of your pages by keeping the typeface simple. Use no more than two font styles. I suggest that whenever possible, you place a single artifact on a single page with a title sized 18 to 36 points. You can make the title or headline bold if you like but avoid other special effects. Then you'll want to add a caption in the same type font, sized at 10 to 14 points, in bold, italic, or plain type style.

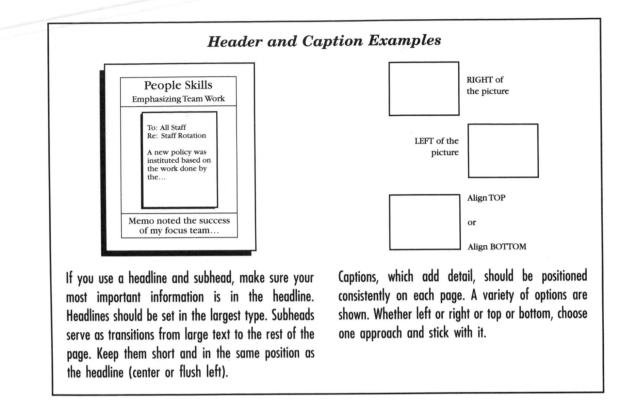

Header and Caption Examples

People Skills
Emphasizing Team Work

To: All Staff
Re: Staff Rotation

A new policy was
instituted based on
the work done by
the...

Memo noted the success
of my focus team...

RIGHT of
the picture

LEFT of the
picture

Align TOP

or

Align BOTTOM

If you use a headline and subhead, make sure your most important information is in the headline. Headlines should be set in the largest type. Subheads serve as transitions from large text to the rest of the page. Keep them short and in the same position as the headline (center or flush left).

Captions, which add detail, should be positioned consistently on each page. A variety of options are shown. Whether left or right or top or bottom, choose one approach and stick with it.

If your smaller caption text will run more than two lines deep (i.e., down the page), consider breaking the text up into two shorter-width columns rather than sending long lines across the entire width of the page; long lines are hard for the eye to follow. As a general guideline, try to keep columns to no more than 40 characters wide.

Most experts believe that serif type has the greatest readability, especially for small and dense body text. Serif type is often used for captions. Never use more than two type styles per page and be consistent with the fonts you use throughout the portfolio.

Other decisions will affect the readability of your text. Avoid using unfamiliar special-effects type such as dashes (—) and ellipses (. . .). Similarly, try not to shout everything in capital letters. In fact, headlines are easier to read in lower case with the first letter of each word capitalized. If a headline must span more than one line, first try to shorten it by editing. If that fails, break the headline into logical phrases or word groups. Try not to end a line with prepositions or adjectives.

STRIVE FOR SIMPLICITY

In the end, strive for visual unity and consistency. If you use color, know its implication. Black connotes elegance and sophistication and red suggests

Typography Examples

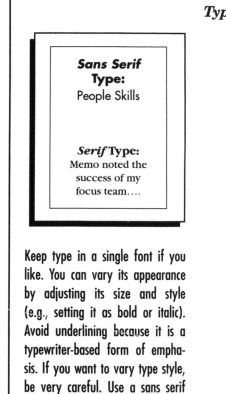

**Sans Serif
Type:**
People Skills

***Serif* Type:**
Memo noted the
success of my
focus team....

Keep type in a single font if you like. You can vary its appearance by adjusting its size and style (e.g., setting it as bold or italic). Avoid underlining because it is a typewriter-based form of emphasis. If you want to vary type style, be very careful. Use a sans serif font for titles and captions and a serif font for body text.

This is Sans Serif, Bold at 14 Pt.
(straight line type)
This is Sans Serif, Bold at 10 Pt.

This is Serif, Bold at 14 Pt.
(type with little serifs or extensions at the ends of lines)
This is Serif, Bold at 10 Pt.

Sometimes you can put type in a reverse field, as when using white type on a black background. Only do this when you can use large type, preferably 14 points or larger. Sans serif is easier to read in reverse than serif.

excitement, power, and energy, while green conjures up nature, fun, or casual attitudes. Try to match the color to the image you wish to project. Likewise, on any given page try to create a consistent "texture" when using artwork. For instance, avoid combining line drawings or sketches with photographs and other three-dimensional representations. If you are using an identifying logo, place it consistently on each page in a corner or near a margin, preferably somewhere on the bottom half of the page. Finally, hold back—don't add anything extra. Avoid highlighting a word with color because color turns a word that's meant to be read into a decorative element. Avoid decoration with color, type styles, or icons.

One way to achieve simplicity is to work with the white space as part of your design; use it to draw your reader's eye to the main event. If your page appears cluttered or too busy, remove the distracting object(s) or crop (cut down) the object to reduce its size. You need to have at least a 1-inch border of white space on your page.

All of these principles can be applied to both paper and the computer screen. If you want to produce your portfolio on computer, lay it out on paper first and then translate it into a digital computer format. Working out the design on paper

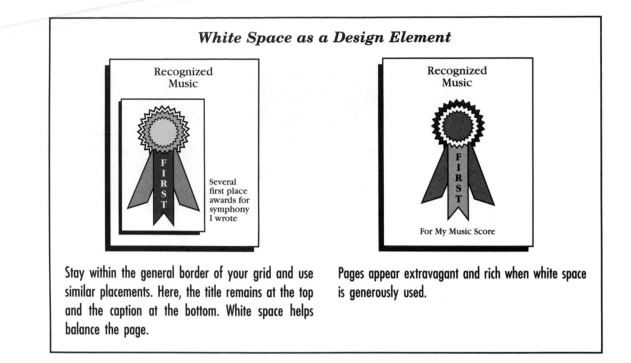

White Space as a Design Element

Recognized Music

F I R S T

Several first place awards for symphony I wrote

Recognized Music

F I R S T

For My Music Score

Stay within the general border of your grid and use similar placements. Here, the title remains at the top and the caption at the bottom. White space helps balance the page.

Pages appear extravagant and rich when white space is generously used.

will help you focus on layout principles. Once you get to the computer screen, you can easily be distracted by choices about color, buttons, linking, and other commands, but if your page is already designed on paper, the aesthetics won't get lost in the process of using the software. Remember to use the computer to simplify the presentation, not complicate it.

FRONT MATTER—DO IT LAST

As you put the last work sample page into your portfolio, it's time to turn to the front. I recommend doing the front matter last because it's easier to write it once you've already got your contents organized. Front matter typically includes the title page, acknowledgments, table of contents, and introduction.

This front matter material will vary in length depending on the kind of portfolio and the needs of your audience. In a portfolio organized to meet specific criteria (for a scholarship, college credit, loan application, or a performance review) the introductory material must conform to specific guidelines. The introduction in a performance review portfolio may need to address the connection between the individual's performance and the organization's mission, goals, and training programs. One might be asked to provide an overview or list of contributions to the organization, the areas of study, the skills to be mastered, and goals for professional and personal growth.

There are many possible ways to write an introduction. Hopefully your language, sense of order, and style will reflect your personality. There is nothing worse than reading résumés or portfolio introductions that all sound like they were written by the same person.

If the portfolio is to be used for job seeking, then I'd recommend crafting an introduction that is part cover letter, part résumé. When developing one for a specific employer, it is important to state how your career objectives and experiences match the job position. In this regard, the portfolio resembles a targeted résumé and cover letter. Remember, you can revise this introduction to fit each employer. If you are assembling a more general-purpose portfolio in anticipation of future interviews, then keep the language global rather than limited to the lingo of a specific employer.

In a portfolio organized chronologically, it is helpful to sum up the most significant sections and highlight the individual samples representing major turning points in your life. The same applies to a portfolio organized around functional categories. In addition, a short history helps address the portfolio reader's interests in knowing what you have done over time. This compensates for the lack of dates found mostly in chronological portfolios. The portfolio organized around themes deserves a slightly different approach. Use the introduction to explain the meaning behind certain thematic phrases. In other words, define your terms. Relate the thematic headings to specific experiences in work, training, and personal life.

You may also want to discuss how various portfolio artifacts demonstrate different temperaments or work habits, similar to the ideas found in Appendix D: Personality Words. The portfolio is far richer than a two-page résumé or a dry and dull job application because it carries your unique imprint.

As you set about writing the introduction, tailor the length and style to the needs of your audience and the time you think they will have for reviewing your portfolio. You can use the following suggestions as benchmarks, but don't consider these as absolutes. When writing an introduction for a personal portfolio, think of it as a letter to yourself. There are no limits on length, but three to five pages will usually suffice.

An introduction to a professional portfolio must be the epitome of brevity. Keep it short when writing for busy employers or clients. Somewhere between one-half to a full page is probably satisfactory. Don't make it eye-tiring; use 12-point type and generous margins. If there's room, set the lines at one-and-one-half or double space.

If you plan to leave the portfolio with the interviewer, then you may want to write a richer introduction that can be read at a later time, instead of merely skimmed during the interview. This longer introduction might run two or five pages. Educational institutions generally want an introduction that runs three to five pages.

Take a look at the samples on the next two pages, designed to help you write your introduction. Since some people learn best when given a model while others prefer a step-by-step set of directions, I've provided one of each.

You may use the first person (the pronoun "I") in your introduction, but don't overuse it—not more than three or four times in a paragraph. Instead of beginning with the phrase "I have had experience in . . ." rework the word order and language using something like "My experience in XYZ clearly demonstrates. . . ." Since it is obvious that you are referring to your own experiences, you can sometimes leave direct references to yourself out if you find yourself beginning to overuse the word "I." Instead of writing "I earned my Ph.D. and then went into . . . " you could start with "After earning a Ph.D., several executive recruiters made contact."

A PORTFOLIO HIGHLIGHTS SUMMARY

It cannot be said too often: There is never any single correct way to do a portfolio. Some have used a letter format, others a memo, and still others a narrative or storytelling style. Roger von Oech, a leading author on creativity, suggests that truly creative thinking begins when you look for multiple answers to a problem. With this in mind, you might come up with your own unique approach to front matter.

For instance, you may be able to combine the indexing feature of a table of contents with the summarizing quality of a résumé to create what I call a Portfolio Highlights Summary. It is akin to writing a synopsis of your portfolio, and it can include dates as well as page numbers. An example of this kind of summary is shown on page 135.

Notice that the summary uses a two-column format. In the left-hand column, you'll find short titles or phrases. They act like headlines, drawing the eye for a quick read. In the right-hand column, additional details are given. The reader is drawn to the facts, which serve as mini-summaries. Each summary should begin with a key word describing the artifact, followed by an explanation written in descriptive language.

The author of this summary intentionally limited the sample portfolio to six items. As a result, it was not necessary to divide the portfolio into sections or chapters. Think of this portfolio as one that includes only the most impressive samples from each section of a larger portfolio. The section descriptions, which normally might come before a number of related artifacts, become the basis for the summaries on this highlights page. If your experience is limited or intermittent, I suggest using only page numbers; leave off the dates.

The Portfolio Highlights Summary, which can be effectively used in short portfolios, can also double as a résumé.

Artifact #5

Sample introduction for a professional portfolio

Youth Community Service Portfolio: Introduction and Highlights

This portfolio illustrates a wide range of skills that are well-suited to the present position of Youth Community Service Department Coordinator. The final candidate must possess a nonpartisan image and a multitude of talents if the fragmented viewpoints and various strands are to be successfully woven together into a meaningful community initiative.

Section 1—Problem Solving

The samples in this section demonstrate my ability to define problems, develop research or information-gathering, and synthesize findings into a meaningful report or presentation. Work samples include research documents, focus group questionnaires, strategic planning charts, and quotations showing how community service can greatly enhance the efforts to rebuild our communities.

Section 2—Visualizing the Future

Various pages from my report *Imagine* make up the majority of this section. This report was widely read and praised for its comprehensive quality and specific program suggestions. The strategic plan summarized the assets and related benefits of community youth service; challenges and suggestions noted by practitioners; and strategic options for transforming the practice of community service from an exceptional event into an everyday experience. I enjoyed the project because it allowed me the chance to use my writing and desktop publishing skills.

Section 3—Getting the Message Across

I used contacts made on the Internet and through in-person networking. A list of the 300+ people interviewed is included. A hard-copy printout illustrates how the resulting database of over 300 people can be used in the future to pinpoint essential community links. Moreover, the photos show various presentations in which I used my public speaking and training skills during testimony before the state legislature and at workshops and conferences.

Overall, the work samples testify to my efforts at developing a unified vision for a field that has historically been fragmented by the different funding sources and practices (related to programs in schools, private agencies, business, labor, and public nonprofit agencies). I believe this portfolio demonstrates that I possess the talents and experience necessary for coordinating and implementing programs funded by the new federal dollars earmarked for community development. I can contribute the vision, contacts, and leadership qualities needed to forge a new community service initiative involving our youth.

Outline for a Portfolio Introduction

1. **In the first few lines, state the purpose of the portfolio; tell what you are trying to prove or demonstrate. Some examples follow:**

   - This portfolio demonstrates my lifelong involvement with social services . . .
   - The documents in my portfolio provide evidence of competent and innovative programming in the field of social service for which I am seeking credit in various sociology classes.
   - My portfolio illustrates how I can contribute to the organization's competitive edge in the XYZ arena . . .
   - My entrepreneurial talents will ensure that this new business venture will reap rewards for all who invest.
   - Samples in this portfolio demonstrate how I can bring to market a product that will . . .

2. **Briefly sum up your experiences or advantages and relate them to the audience (or job), if possible.**

   I have over ten years experience and training in the XYZ occupation. My studies began at XYZ university and my first job was with ABC agency. I was promoted from position M to position N in two years. My next job at UVW gave me a broader perspective on the need to develop JKL in our field. I believe that my experiences make me particularly well-suited for the position of XYZ. I can bring to the table my proven experience as well as a strong desire for constant improvement and innovation.

3. **Sum up the contents in each section or highlight the most significant artifacts, being as succinct as possible.**

   The artifacts in this portfolio are cataloged into four categories: Training, Technical Skills, Management Experiences, and Awards and Recognition. Each area contains actual samples or replicas from my life's work. In addition, letters attesting to my competence and quality of performance are also included along with work samples. The complete sample or original artifact can be made available for your examination upon request.

Highlights Summary

Training—This section includes my early teacher evaluations that speak to my industrious nature. Subsequent course transcripts indicate advanced studies and the list of workshops show that I enjoy keeping up with my profession. The final evaluation is from a training event I was asked to conduct.

Technical Skills—This includes samples from my work at ABC Inc. The production schedule, budget analysis, and report cover are samples of my communication and planning abilities. The photograph and blueprints describe how we rearranged our workplace to maximize output. The "Priority Equipment List" articulates the technologies I was responsible for researching, purchasing, and later supporting. My support-services schedule shows how I coordinated training of the staff.

Management Experiences—Highlighted agendas from management team meetings show my continuing input into the policy process. Newsletter clips from the company describe various programs I have helped to plan or coordinate to benefit our customers. The list of committees indicates my expanding knowledge of operations.

Awards and Recognition—The letters of commendation and awards testify to my untiring efforts to either improve my own skills or the workplace as a whole. I am particularly proud of the 1996 Employee Recognition award since its presentation depends on peer review and acclamation.

Portfolio Highlights Summary

Talents Highlights	Samples and Description
Leadership Skills . . . . Page 3	AVA Co-Chair Picture at Podium where I directed the state's largest professional organization serving career counselors. Spokane, Washington State Conference. 1995.
Communicator and Motivator . . . . . . Page 5	Cassette tape from the Fall 1997 Future's Conference keynote presentation. Later, I was asked to deliver this as a keynote address. Fall, 1997.
Emphasis on Quality . . . . Page 6	Program Evaluation and Quality Control report demonstrates accountability to standards of performance and high levels of customer satisfaction. My methods were later adopted as recommended policy for ASTD. Spring, 1997.
Community Service . . . . Page 8	Community Caring brochure established our reputation as a firm that cares. Our service helped immigrant job seekers who normally go unserved. Winter, 1996.
Self-Directed Learner . . . . Page 10	Learning collage demonstrates my lifelong passion for learning and my natural curiosity. I'm always alert to new trends, which helps in creative problem solving. This project was completed in a workshop conducted by nationally known leader in creative problem solving, Bellah Bolles. Summer 1997.
Multilingual . . . . Page 11	Poem in Spanish shows my pride in my heritage. Subsequent samples in Japanese and Russian illustrate my language ability. This poem was selected for publication in *El Trabador* in 1995.

Your Closing Reflection

Portfolios created for public school and college credit usually end with a reflection or concluding piece. The pupils are asked to evaluate their final product and the actual experience of making the portfolio. If you are asked for one, or if you like this effect and want to use one in your portfolio, keep it brief. While it may repeat major ideas from the introduction, try to add some new materials or a new perspective.

In a job-search portfolio, you could reiterate your goals from the front and then mention the larger themes that animate your life or your career journey. If you are doing this for an educational institution, you could describe how you felt after completing the portfolio, the interesting experiences you had while archiving and researching, and the new insights gained about yourself. While a professional portfolio often doesn't need a self-evaluation document, the personal portfolio, in my opinion, should always end with an epilogue or concluding piece.

PORTFOLIO CONSTRUCTION TIPS

As I mentioned earlier, you'll want to provide for maximum flexibility when assembling your portfolio. If you're pasting up your portfolio by hand, use a pliable adhesive such as rubber cement. Use it sparingly in order to simplify the later possible removal and transfer of objects. (If you are making a desktop-published version, then most of your artwork and displays can be scanned and moved about at will.) Try to output your hard copy on a quality printer that provides high resolution and several levels of gray; otherwise you risk losing some of the visual details.

People often ask how to fit in everything (the title, caption, and large artifacts) without winding up with a large bulky document. I have three suggestions:

1. You can use legal-size paper in the portfolio because it is longer than the standard 8½ × 11 page and, thus, provides additional room for titles and captions at the top and bottom of the page.

2. You can use reduced-size copies or photographs of large and bulky three-dimensional objects (ribbons, medals, disks, cassettes, bound works). Take your original items to a high-quality copy service and have them make copies at a 15 to 20 percent reduction. The reduced items then allow room at the top and bottom for titles and captions.
   If you think an artifact will lose it's readability or important detail if it is reduced, then you have two additional options. Use a significantly reduced picture as an icon representing the object, with a caption like, "A full-size replica of this object is found on the following page (or appendix)," or "A full-size version of this item is available for examination upon request."

3. You can group all commentary and captions on a separate single page, thereby freeing up the entire page for the artifact. Try clustering similar artifacts into common sections or chapters. Then, place a summary statement before each section that essentially includes the captions you would normally have near each artifact.

Writing Summary Statements for Portfolio Sections

A sample introductory passage from a section of my professional portfolio is shown in Artifact #6. It sums up what I am trying to say with the subsequent samples. In it, I explain the interdisciplinary approach I take, integrating my

---

Artifact #6
Sample introduction to a portfolio section or chapter

The Interdisciplinary Life

Today the words "integrated studies" and "interdisciplinary teaching teams" have come into vogue. I hope they stay in our vocabulary, because I have enjoyed integrating many different interests during my lifelong studies. Today I possess over fifteen notebooks on my studies.

As factory worker, artist, and teacher, I have constantly integrated the themes of technology, art, and education in both my teaching and personal life. I am fascinated by the interplay of work and leisure opportunities, how one activity leads to a job, and how a job leads to exploring new tools and techniques for leisure.

---

nonschool life experiences into my teaching. It contains samples showing how I utilize drama, art, technology, and community outreach together in my studies and teaching. You can see that I've created a heading for this sectional page; even when using a page devoted to summaries or captions, I still recommend finding some way to put a title, a heading, or short captions on each page containing an artifact.

Final Draft, Language Checklist

Before you put down your pen or turn off the word processor and begin the final stages of construction, review what you have written in your captions, introduction, and other front matter. You'll want to make your language vivid, engaging, and polished. Use the following checklist before settling on your final text:

- **Keep the tense consistent and the writing brief**

  If possible try to write in the present tense and be succinct. "The certificate represents my efforts at fund-raising" is a better caption than the more wordy "This certificate was awarded for my past fund-raising results and diligent recruitment efforts." If you find that most of your statements work best in the past tense (since they represent past accomplishments), then use the past tense throughout. Keep tense consistent and strive to weed out wordiness in your writing.

- **Keep the language you use in an active rather than passive voice.**

  This includes trying to avoid using the words *is*, *was*, and *were* that make sentences wordy or less direct. If you are unsure about this, ask an English teacher or editor to review your writing or to coach you.

- **Beware of using clichés or jargon people won't understand.**

Ask others to read and point out unclear language.

- **Watch for potentially offensive language.**

Experiences linked to religious or political organizations may raise a red flag. If you must mention the church newsletter, emphasize the size and scope of the venture and minimize or leave out the name of the organization. For instance, you might write, "This newsletter was distributed to over 200 members of a local church group. It came out biweekly, and we never missed a deadline." Ask at least two other people to review your material for potentially offensive language (sexism, ageism, racism, etc.).

- **Avoid acronyms and abbreviations unless you are certain your readers will know what they are.**

- **Avoid making all captions sound alike.**

Vary your language. Consult the Appendixes for ideas about words, and use a thesaurus.

- **Use your computer's spell checker,** and then read what you've written carefully out loud again. Better yet, have at least one other person do a final proofing.

Paper, Sheet Protectors

Colored paper can also enhance the visual unity of your product. Perhaps the artifacts related to travel could be mounted on green paper, computer skills on blue, and management experiences on yellow. A light pink page might be used as a divider before each major section and should contain a title for the subsequent section or chapter. This way you can tell at a glance where different sections begin.

I once tried to update an old portfolio, but I couldn't match the color of the paper ten years later. All the samples had to be removed and remounted. To save yourself agony later, buy at least a half ream of each color so that you'll have plenty when you want to revise your portfolio later. If colored paper is not to your liking, try creating a logo using an icon or use special-display text fonts to link similar exhibits in a given chapter.

Once a page is complete with mounted artifact, title, and caption, I place it in a plastic envelope. These envelopes are generally called sheet protectors and can be found in any office supply store. The plastic envelopes not only protect your portfolio pages, they also solve a page-numbering problem. In the past, I found it difficult to add new pages or change the order of pages because it meant I had to print new paper with new page numbers and paste or repaste the artifacts. Then I came up with a better idea of placing page numbers on the plastic sheet protectors. The plastic envelopes remain in the binder, in the same order, but their contents change. I just shift the samples back and forth as needed and adjust the table of contents or section summaries. This way, I avoid putting page numbers on the actual page holding the artifact and text. Try handwriting or printing out the numbers on self-adhesive labels or purchase stick-on number decals. A typical table of contents entry could include:

Workshops and Seminars . . . blue . . . pages 9 to 12.

It might be helpful to visit an art supply store to get more ideas. Examine books about making art portfolios. You may wish to consult Ed Marquand's book *How To Prepare Your Portfolio*, written for designers and artists. It contains information about paper stock, acetone and plastic protector sheets, mat boards, lamination, cutting techniques, photostats, half tones, and photocopying techniques.

12

THE FINAL REVIEW

Evaluating Your Completed Portfolio

▶ Earlier in this book, you took a moment to analyze the needs of your audience. This served as a guide in selecting the final content for the finished portfolio. Now, as your portfolio nears completion, consider your audience one more time.

- Have you arrived at the point you set out for?

- Does the portfolio say and demonstrate what you thought it would?

- How do you think readers will react to it?

Each person who views your portfolio will consciously or unconsciously evaluate its content, look, and feel. Employers, in particular, will compare your "product" against their standards or expectations. The final question is "Does your portfolio successfully market your talents?"

This is the same question skilled résumé writers ask before heading off to the printer. They use checklists to guide their assessment of the product's final appearance, organization, and content. But unlike résumés, there are no generally accepted formats or standards for portfolios. This is new territory. Therefore, you'll need to design a checklist that allows you to review your final product, as well as get feedback from others.

Before showing the portfolio to prospective employers or other strangers who will be looking at it critically, it's a good idea to get feedback about your product and presentation from people you know. You may wish to get input from instructors, members of professional organizations, career counselors, or people working in your field. This last reality test will help to ensure that your information and artifacts are on target and that your presentation is impressive.

USING A SCORING RUBRIC

A good way to test your finished portfolio is with a rubric. This evaluation tool is nothing more than a listing of criteria that allows you to rate each portfolio quality on a scale rather than a single checklist box that requires an all-or-nothing, yes/no response. The rubric requires that you look at many different dimensions: content, aesthetics, message, organization. This approach addresses the complex and subjective task of evaluating the multiple media represented by artifacts as well as words. Using a scale is also important because when you ask others to judge your product, they will be more comfortable using a scale rather than a thumbs-up or thumbs-down checklist.

▶ EXERCISE #13
Evaluating Your Portfolio with a Rubric

If you were in charge of designing a portfolio evaluation sheet, what elements would you want assessed? What should a top-quality portfolio in your field look like? Take a look at the sample rubric on the next page; it contains some general criteria applicable for any portfolio. Then see if you can customize the rubric to your field of interest by adding a few additional criteria in the left-hand column blanks.

These additional criteria should be based on what you think your audience will be looking for. If you are unsure about what is expected for your professional portfolio, consider asking people who work in your field or train others in it if they have time to help evaluate your portfolio. Let these experts score it and then compare it to your own self-evaluation.

Each criterion on the left is evaluated from a top score of 3 to low score of 1. A 3 simply means that you have met the criteria or that you have achieved a polished, finished state. A score of 1 means you are still at the working or draft state, and revision will be necessary. A score of 2 allows someone to score you with a sense of doubt. It is wise to ask your evaluators to suggest how to move a score of a 1 or 2 up to a 3.

A FINAL CHECK OF YOUR LANGUAGE AND GOALS

Résumé experts have always cautioned job hunters to thoroughly review their résumés to insure that the skills and experiences listed support the stated career

Portfolio Evaluation Rubric

Elements and Criteria to Evaluate	Competitive or Polished Level 3	Formative or Emerging Level 2	Draft or Working Level 1
Aesthetics			
Eye-Appeal	Uncluttered, pleasing to the eye	Too much on a page	Too much on a page
Consistency	Consistent placement on pages	Too much variety, but still can be followed	Must hunt to find page number, captions, or commentary
Organization and flow	Clean, easy to view	Somewhere in between	Messy or sloppy
Documented Character Traits and Work Habits			
Being responsible, self-directed, taking initiative			
Ability to get along, team player			
Problem solving			
Documented Technical Skills			
Look at a job description and pick out the 3 most important duties			
List an essential knowledge or training you have			
Think about current fads or trends such as			
List essential skill or talent that may help you on the job			

goal at the top of the page. Too often, extraneous or superfluous material is included. For instance, you don't need to list your educational experience if you have been out of school for ten or more years.

If your goal is to change careers from the private to the nonprofit sector or go from military to civilian work, then you'll need to downplay those work experiences that don't translate well into the new field. Military background needs to be recast in civilian terms (see chapter 7), and profit-oriented experiences may need to be worded in the language of the nonprofit sector. When interviewing for the public sector, talk about generating clients or saving costs rather than generating market share or making profits.

Getting the language right for your audience means that you must be precise and clear and that you give enough detail without using little-known jargon. A caption reading "This letter shows that I enjoy working with people" is far too general, even flabby. After all, both a teacher and a mortician could make the same statement! On the other hand, a caption claiming, "My VMET transcripts show the ability to articulate and process command protocols" would mean nothing to the average civilian. One has to be specific enough to convince while avoiding vernacular, technical babble, and acronyms that may not be shared by your audience.

You can always show your portfolio to people in the field you hope to enter and ask them, "Which parts or language did you find clear and impressive, and which parts appeared vague or unimpressive?" Try to get at least two or three opinions before making final changes, and then make only changes that feel right and appear to be corroborated by at least one other person.

Similarly, you must make sure that your artifacts support your claims and career goals. One expert in employment portfolios tells the story of a job seeker applying to work in her office. The applicant showed up with pay stubs from her last job in local government. She pointed to the column listing the number of accumulated sick-leave days and contended that it showed excellent attendance. However, her prospective employer, who had worked the same number of years in government, had accumulated three times the sick leave! This employer figured that the job seeker's sense of good attendance did not match the expectations of the office, and the interview quickly ground to a halt.

Taking a Critical Look

As you look over your finished product, ask yourself, "Do my artifacts demonstrate that I understand expectations and professional standards related to this job or place of work?" You might also ask yourself, "Could any of my artifacts be considered superfluous or even contradictory?"

Up to this point, you have looked at the aesthetics and the documentation of your product. Now you need to shift your perspective, stand back, and look at the product from the viewpoint of a stranger, possibly the person who will be evaluating you at an interview. The critical question becomes: How will your portfolio impress a stranger who is looking at this portfolio for the first time? Supporting questions to consider include:

- Is my language clear and detailed, and are technical terms fully explained?

- Have I translated my experiences into the language of the employer?

- Do my artifacts support my career goal?

To address these questions, you may wish to add the following two categories about wording and goals to your Portfolio Evaluation Rubric.

Portfolio Evaluation Rubric Additions

Wording and Clarity		
Have you cast your skills in terms your audience will understand? (Interpret skills in the language of your reader: nonprofit, government, business, civilian perspective)		
Have you explained any specialized or technical terms? Did you explain acronyms?		
Goals and Artifacts Match		
Does every artifact support your career goal?		

13

THE VIRTUAL PORTFOLIO

Creating and Using an Electronic Portfolio

▶ Log on and you enter the virtual universe called cyberspace; don a funny set of video goggles and fill your cranium with virtual reality. Seek medical information, share a lesson plan, or gather advice about relationships or finances and you've joined hands across logic boards in today's virtual community. The digital Disneyland is challenging the way we do business, communicate, form communities, and perceive reality. It is logical to assume that this new digital reality will also affect portfolios—transforming them from collections of three-dimensional objects into multimedia documents that fuse text, sound, and visual imagery.

Let us digress in this chapter and project for the moment into the future employment world of the late twenty-second century. . . .

In this *Star Trek* universe, you use an Infobot to manage your career. This information-seeking robot uploads your preferences and talents and then trolls oceans of megadata for jobs or projects matching your interests and talents. When it finds an opportunity that matches your goals, it posts a message back home that it's time to revise your profile in light of a possible job opportunity. Your Infobot regularly attends a Robot Academy to keep up with the ever-changing infrastructure of cyberspace; it collects new key words, tips about job hunting, and gossip from other Infobots.

Taken with a grain of salt and a dash of humor, such forecasting helps expand the sense of what is possible, especially once you realize that the roots of most predictions are often firmly planted in the soils of the present. We don't yet have Infobots, but people are working today on scripted programs that scan on-line newspaper articles for you, selecting what is pertinent to your interests. Prototypes of this kind of intelligence-gathering have been dubbed *smart agents* that act on your behalf, supposedly learning your interests, and then going out and seeking information that matches them.

Telecommunications expert Leni Donlan spends many hours managing several on-line education projects and co-coordinates the Electronic School House on the America Online network. She made the following observation about our journey toward a digital job-search future:

> *Already, savvy Internauts are using Infobots to collect and screen information. News-reading software scans newsgroup postings and collects all articles that contain specified key words and phrases, then automatically sends them to the user's electronic mailbox. Sophisticated electronic-mail software screens incoming mail and separates this mail into discrete groupings. Web publishers are producing displays that incorporate multimedia as well as text-based information to share with the world at large.*

(Note: *A Web site* uses a *home page* that operates like a multimedia document. You click on highlighted key words, pictures, or buttons—called *hypertext links*, or *links*—to get additional information. Thus, the home page is linked to other documents that you choose to read in any order.)

Within the next few years, it will be possible to exchange almost any kind of information in almost any form with users of any platform. The possibilities here are enormous as new tools and solutions appear daily, allowing us to create and share in ways never possible before!

Executive recruiter Bill Vick created Recruiters On-line Network, an on-line clearinghouse for positions and information that is available only to professional recruiters in both permanent and temporary employment agencies. Vick's electronic forum can accelerate the hunt capabilities of placement specialists who can now draw from a much larger pool of information. This is critical when the search for talent must measure up to the very detailed and demanding criteria supplied by employers looking for six-figure income candidates. Bill Vick feels that this kind of connecting service will eventually branch out to mainstream employment operations: "I see yesterday's résumé being replaced by a new medium much richer in content. I believe that portfolios, as I understand them, are going to become critical in the new work mentality."

Today, applicants are increasingly asked to demonstrate talents through participation in performance interviews. For instance, an interviewee might be asked to give evidence of communication skills by delivering an impromptu speech, demonstrate people skills by chairing a goal-setting focus group, or exhibit the ability to use a particular technical skill in a hands-on problem-solving event.

In the future, observing the performance of candidates could be done with three-dimensional holographs. Where once job seekers pasted photos on their résumé, tomorrow's multimedia portfolio will come packaged with much more. You'll be able to upload a home page on the Internet with your name, summary of talents, and even an animated picture showing you at work—accompanied by the jazzy sounds of your favorite music.

SPECULATING ABOUT THE FUTURE OF VIRTUAL PORTFOLIOS

Computers are playing an increasingly important role in helping employers find the talent they need. Even now, some of the larger, more technologically sophisticated companies are using software that can scan résumés for key words that indicate skills, education, or past employment of interest to the employer. Where once the job seeker had to get past the secretary, now he or she must make it past the software! In the future, electronic portfolios may be forwarded to a review committee or search team for further evaluation.

In this nearly here future, an employer will call up the applicant's Web page, which serves as a table of contents to various artifacts existing in digital format. Reviewers will point and click or speak words that trigger hot buttons on the first virtual page. Clicking on the button labeled *Commendations* transfers the document to other pages containing scanned images of awards. Selecting, next, the button tagged *Problem Solving* whisks the reader to budget spreadsheets and organization charts illustrating how the job seeker helped plan for budget cuts and workplace restructuring. One button will take the viewer to a time line showing accomplishments, another might start a video clip of a speech, a third will read aloud a sample representing the candidate's writing skills.

Many forecasters predict that the World Wide Web will some day become as common as television in most homes. If this becomes true, we are on the threshold of a change that will make the Web the perfect medium for the professional electronic portfolio. The electronic portfolio offers many different samples without overwhelming the employer with a 3-inch ring binder. Web pages allow the reviewer to look for information that is most relevant—in the blink of a mouse click.

As this reality takes shape, résumé-writing services may go the way of the typing pool. When it's time to update your portfolio and résumé, you'll make an appointment at a digital portfolio studio. Here you'll stage scenes for the camera, demonstrate various technical skills or products, scan significant documents, and digitize pictures of three-dimensional artifacts as you construct your professional multimedia job-search kit. It's possible that you (or perhaps your children) will find a future job through a computer network. An employer could request a digital sample, or multimedia portfolio, of your work. The decision to hire may be made in your community or halfway around the world. Your interview might be conducted via videoconference with a panel of examiners hundreds or even thousands of miles away, while you sit in front your personal computer enhanced with a video camera.

The foundation for this future is being laid today. We have multimedia software headhunters looking for talent on the Internet, and Joyce Lain Kennedy and other on-line career experts have written books explaining how employers currently use computers to screen job applicant résumés. The government-run job-service centers are trying to speed the matching of employers and job seekers with user-friendly databases and touch screens. Huge communications and computer corporations have joined in strategic alliances to invest megabucks in developing services that connect people through their video screens. The World Wide Web will undoubtedly have a profound impact on the way job searches are played out in the future—it's not a question of if, but when.

Of course, while much of this section about virtual portfolios is riddled with conjecture, we really don't know what form job seeking will finally take in our increasingly computerized world. We just know it will change, along with everything else.

Despite all these high-technology ventures, paper résumés, portfolios, and in-person interviews will remain the dominant medium of exchange for quite some time. As anyone who has recently logged onto the Internet knows, we are only in the infancy of the digital job search. In fact, as I write these words, I still cannot easily send a decently formatted document from my Macintosh computer to a person using an IBM PC or another platform. As a result, much of the computer-mediated communication going on now needs to be limited to plain-vanilla text files, without pictures, audio, or formatting.

This digression into sci-fi job hunting serves several purposes. First, you begin to think beyond today's technology when planning a portfolio. Second, it suggests that we all need to connect with the current technology in some fashion if we are to flourish in the future. And last, we must try to make the portfolio both employer-friendly and computer-friendly. That is, while you might be designing plain text files for uploading in the 1990s, don't forget to save (or conceptualize ways you might send) digitized samples of pictures, sound, and representations of actual work on a video clip.

Case Study—Employment Portfolio Web Site Under Construction

In the mid-1990s, Patrik and Peter Muzila began designing a Web site that they hoped would offer a speedy digital alternative to the costly and time-consuming system of matching employers with job seekers. They started with the notion of setting up an on-line résumé database. However, they soon felt the need to go beyond résumé publishing if their product was to reflect the truly dynamic nature of job-changing in our times. The brothers concluded that the complexity of careers in the late twentieth century could be best portrayed at a Web site with multimedia potential. While only a rudimentary display of what may be possible down the road, their vision captures the possibilities.

The brothers began with the concept of a digital résumé, and this grew into a digital folder that would enable people to store a constantly changing set of information describing their education, skills, abilities, and preferences. Their *Portfolio Manager* became the basis of the Muzila brothers' Web site, JobTailor. It is a database that strives to capture the open-ended nature of a portfolio. Unlike traditional on-line résumé databases, JobTailor users are not limited to a single page or form; they can continuously expand and update their information. This database combines some of the best features of portfolios and résumés.

To enter the JobTailor database, a user logs on, then selects a password. Next he completes various parts, or records, in the database. These records include standard types of information sought by employers such as work history, skills, preferences (location and pay), and addresses (that can be kept confidential). In addition, a free-form record allows the user to enter just about any description of his or her talents. For instance, a graphic artist could enter key words related to computer graphics, 2-D graphics, print media, direct mail, or any other skills.

Use Both a High- and Low-Tech Strategy to Maximize Compatibility

The current problems of computer and network compatibility sometimes rivals the challenge of achieving human compatibility. Neither is easy. What's a body to do while we wait for the computer industry to simplify our electronic communications?

Create two versions of everything, a high- and low-tech version.

First, strip your digital résumé or portfolio down to a plain vanilla version, based on the assumption that the other party may be using a minimum (or a less than compatible) computer configuration. This means a plain ASCII text file. Then, create a second version decked out with all the high-tech bells and whistles at your disposal. Send the well-endowed version to people who share the same software and hardware as you.

I have used this principle successfully whenever I upload items on-line such as lessons, essays, books, or plays. I always send up a text version along with a fully formatted version. This gives people a choice for downloading. In addition, I sometimes offer to send a hard copy version by adding the following line to a plain text résumé or portfolio: "An attractive and fully formatted hard copy version of this document is available upon request."

Having a text version provides you with additional insurance. Suppose after putting all that hard work into creating a portfolio Web page, you finally receive an invitation to a job interview. You arrive, only to find that their computer system is down or the employer is not on-line. That's why you bring along either a hard copy or a portable laptop loaded with your portfolio Web site. The paper copy can be left behind as a reminder. Infonaut Phil Shapiro frequently uses a variation on this theme. He gives people a disk that contains a copy of his portfolio and the necessary software for viewing the documents. Having more than one version is the key.

When all the records have been completed, a core portfolio of basic information sums up one's experience in conventional résumé categories: *Training, Experience, Awards, Specialty Skills*. Later, when an employer requests portfolios for graphic artists, a list of criteria or skill sets drives the database search for portfolios in JobTailor.

Patrik feels that the interactive nature of the portfolio database serves not only those seeking employment but also a larger base of people who want to actively manage their careers: "Many of our subscribers are already employed and, in many instances, happily employed. These people think of their portfolios as a continuous source of information about themselves and their abilities. We believe that this way of thinking will, in fact, be a crucial element in these people's success in the job market."

As the Internet becomes a true conveyor of multimedia imagery, the possibilities become very exciting. Employers could visit the job seeker's personal Web site to view examples of the skills listed on a résumé or portfolio. In the case of a graphic artist, a personal Web site might include a video clip illustrating an actual ad campaign, pictures of current or award-winning work, sounds from ads or interviews, and scanned images (such as an actual award). As the technology matures, the content could evolve along with it. Perhaps spoken letters of reference will replace text-based artifacts. Click on the *References Available Here* button and a video clip shows the job seeker leading a creative planning session with various clients. A small box displays the supervisor lauding the graphic artist's ability to work with people as well as product.

EFFECTIVE DESIGN FOR ON-LINE COMMUNICATIONS AND PORTFOLIOS

We want out computers and software to be user-friendly but our job-search documents to be computer-friendly. Remember that scanning machines, rather than people, may be reading your résumé or the job-search cover letter that mentions your portfolio. As electronic mail (e-mail) increasingly replaces surface mail, you need to learn how to use this medium for both correspondence and networking.

Strategies for all these areas will be discussed next, including various design and formatting methods that will prevent you from being rejected based on computer incompatibility or aesthetic shortcomings. You don't want your efforts to be dismissed simply because you used the wrong software approach.

While there are many ways to exchange information on the Internet, e-mail and the World Wide Web are the most common means of communication. You start your Web browsing at a home page, which fills your computer window with a hyperlinked or multimedia document. A page contains highlighted key words, pictures, or buttons called hypertext links (or links for short) because they are linked electronically to additional information elsewhere online. When you click on these hypertext links, you are instantly transported to supporting documents or other sites on the Internet. As a result, you select the information you want, viewing it in the order you choose.

The software used to view a home page is called a *browser.*

> ## It's Still A Paper World
>
> Margaret F. Riley, author of *The PLA Guide to Internet Job Searching*, reported that after posting her résumé with the Online Career Center, she received twenty-six phone calls, two letters, and no e-mail. Thus, one should never use the Internet alone but rather as an additional tool to the traditional and proven methods of relying on paper products and personal contacts.

Web pages are designed using computer codes known as HTML (Hyper Text Markup Language). Because the Web is easy to use and interactive, it is generally believed that this form of communication may rival the usefulness of print, telephone, and current forms of television in the future.

Plan on Paper, Then Get the Professional Advice You Need

As time goes on, the human-to-machine interface invariably becomes simpler while the software and hardware grow more powerful. For instance, when setting up a home page on the Internet in 1995, one had to learn the HTML codes and protocols. This task was generally beyond the average computer user's inclination or talent. By the end of 1996, Wide World Web software called page editors made designing your own home page almost as simple as using a word processor.

Even as the techniques becomes more accessible, the art remains. Most people who want to place their digital portfolio on the Internet will probably work with a professional at this stage of the game, just as one might work with a professional résumé writer. The expert will help you to design a home page with visual impact that can be easily read on most computers. Not only can he advise you on the details of uploading but he can also suggest where to upload to get maximum exposure. Hopefully, in the future, you'll be able to visit a portfolio studio and hand over the rough copy to a computer jock who will put your lifework in its proper digital form.

Because paper is still the most popular and accessible medium, begin with a hard-copy or paper version of your digital portfolio. It can always be distributed to everyone, whether they are computer literate or not. In addition, the hard copy serves as a story board or planning medium, and this alone will save you valuable design time. The print copy becomes your paper prototype and back-up. Your paper version can also be used as a follow-up to inquiries and offers.

TIPS FOR TEXT-BASED COMMUNICATION (E-MAIL, POSTINGS, DOCUMENTS)

The sheer breadth of the Internet and on-line services is now legend. Whatever your interests, you can find a group with a similar outlook or passion. Job seekers may want to contact groups of people who share their professional interests (often called Newsgroups and similar to bulletin boards) or join a mailing list of like-minded people (called a Listserv). In the process of sharing, you will often cultivate new friendships, learn the current lingo in a particular industry, and frequently network for tips and leads about upcoming (or existing) job opportunities.

Based on my experience, I advise you to simplify the formatting of e-mail, documents, and postings because the receiver might have a different operating system (MS-DOS, Windows, OS/2, UNIX, Macintosh, etc.) or different text-reading software. What appears on your screen could vary markedly from what the other person sees on his. To insure smooth exchanges, consider these additional pointers for e-mail and text-based communications:

- Use simple fonts and limit the range of type size to 10 to 12 points. Use a common monospaced type font such as Courier.

- Remove all formatting (bold, italic, underline) as well as specialized desktop printing items such as curly quotes, ligatures, ellipses, and em spaces. Different operating systems use different keys, and a curly quote (') on your computer screen might show up as a empty space or box on another person's screen.

- Remove all horizontal or vertical lines, shading, drop caps, and graphics.

- Put a space at the start of every blank line.

- When using e-mail, limit line length to sixty characters; otherwise, lines tend to break or end in odd or random places on another computer screen. To keep scrolling to a minimum, limit the length of your letter to, hopefully, not more than the size of a single standard screen.

- People who get dozens of e-mail letters a day may not fully understand your comments if you are responding to something they wrote a week or two ago. Therefore, it is prudent to copy a few of their lines into your mail when replying. This will help put your words in their proper context and ensure clear communication.

- Compose your work on a word processor, where you can edit and check for spelling and grammar. Then save the file to a plain text, or ASCII, document. This process removes special invisible formatting codes that may show up as indecipherable symbols in another word processing program. Cut and paste or attach the plain text file into your e-mail message.

- Assume that your e-mail and postings will be judged as closely as your other forms of communication. Although grammatical and typographical mistakes are commonly found in on-line communications, mistakes do create an impression. Carefully check your grammar and syntax before posting and mailing your portfolio to anyone you're dealing with professionally, such as in an informational interview or in a job-search campaign. I use a text-reading utility program Text-Edit, which is available as shareware on America Online. This software will read my text out loud, helping me find spelling errors, omissions, and syntax problems. As a result, I catch many more errors than I would by rereading or using the spelling or grammar checker built into my word processing software.

Use Keyword Résumés

One of the most common ways to gather attention on the Net is to post your résumé electronically at various career centers (or career Web sites) on-line. Some employers will search for your digital résumé by using a search engine or a scanner that hunts for key words in posted résumés. To "get found" by a computer, you need to design your résumé around the key words used by employers in your industry. Key words are the nouns that typically describe the technical skills required in a specific job. These words make up the current buzz words, trends, and jargon of your field.

Résumé experts and authors like Joyce Lain Kennedy (*Electronic Résumé Revolution*) and Yana Parker (*Damn Good Résumés*) suggest including critical key words in prominent locations on the résumé. Software sentries looking for teachers, for example, might scan for words like *alternative assessment, project-based teaching,* or *special-education endorsement.* Key words for a financial controller could include *cash flow, refinancing debt, corporate tax filing,* and *accounts receivable.* Scanners also search for people who write about experiences at prestigious schools and companies. General phrases such as *planned weekly projects* or *managed others* may be ignored by scanners.

To make sure you have the right key words, find out as much as you can about prospective readers' interests. Look over the jargon and other key words found on potential employers' Web sites, in articles about the companies, or in profiles written by such companies like Hoovers, Inc., which publishes information about business in a variety of electronic and print media. Once you have an employer's or recruiter's attention, you can advise them to visit your home page for additional information.

Security Considerations on the Net

Gary Morris coordinates a well-designed Career Development Center on-line home page using the Union College Web site (http://www.union.edu). He suggests that if you are posting a portfolio or résumé to a public area such as a Web site or on-line résumé database, then security should always be a consideration.

Morris advises his students to "never include personal or contact information in the body of your résumé." For additional security, you may want to consider not naming current employers or providing names of references. Instead, use descriptors such as "a well-known engineering firm in Texas" or "references from experts in the field of special education." Likewise, you could add the line, "Names, addresses, and phone numbers of individual employers and references will be made available upon request." The interested employer or recruiter can then request this information after you are contacted directly.

Working with Web Pages Today

Reading a Web page is much easier than creating one. This is because the language used in creating such pages (HTML code) is a complex publishing code designed to accommodate many different computers with different display technologies. Consequently, HTML code currently gives only general page directions to the computer's Internet software (called a browser). It identifies pieces of the document such as titles, paragraphs, lines, and gives general instructions for displaying these elements on your screen. HTML code defines the structure of a document but may not precisely determine the layout or exact appearance.

You need to scrupulously follow the HTML code when creating a multimedia portfolio or home page. If you don't adhere to the specifications, your reader could end up viewing something different from what you planned on your screen. That is, while you can lay out the elements of your home page—even specifying the text styles such as bold and italic—it may not transfer that way to the receiver's computer screen. That screen might be smaller or larger, and colors and fonts may be different. As a result, the placement of text and graphics may also differ. This limitation of HTML code impairs readability by humans and machines.

A few experts predict that it may not be long before the majority of employers require applicants to submit résumés or portfolios electronically. As that day approaches, hopefully employers will suggest the software and services (such as Netscape, Pagemill, Microsoft Network, America Online, WordPerfect, Pagemaker) and the format (text file, HTML, etc.) to use. If you are like me and aren't familiar with the HTML code, network, or word processing software, ask others to help you, or wait until things get simpler.

Design Principles for Portfolio Web Pages

The on-line portfolio needs to be much shorter than the traditional multipage paper portfolio. It should resemble the more succinctly crafted résumé. In the time-compressed computer world, people only briefly browse these pages. If your Web page grows beyond five standard screens, then heed the advice of Webmaster Margaret F. Riley, who suggests that you begin your page with a short introduction summarizing your entire Web site. This could be followed by a table of contents, where readers select the content and navigate through your entire site using hot links or buttons. Unfortunately, once a reader begins jumping around, it is easy to loose track of the starting point, and the overall message could be lost. The trick is to have hot buttons on each page that quickly return the reader to the previous page or the home page.

Keep It Simple and Consistent

You should also avoid the temptation to include lots of bells and whistles on your home page. This is not the place to show off your mastery of fancy software features! Producing a fully loaded Web site could result in a circus-poster home page with eye-jarring effects. Even if you could put every cool software gadget on your own page, there is no guarantee that someone else using another computer platform will be able see all the special effects.

As when creating a traditional portfolio, using the same placement grid in your electronic portfolio will ensure consistency from page to page. Consistency in an electronic document also means using the same symbols in each window. For instance, use the same icon, such as a pointing finger for all your hot buttons, to take the reader to other hyperlinked documents. Strive for a consistent color and line scheme in your backgrounds, text, and borders. If possible, try to keep the placement of tables and forms in similar positions, aligned to the same margin.

The design process cannot begin until you define your audience in terms of specific interests and the level of technology it (hopefully) possesses. This will guide you in selecting and editing the final documents for a Web page. For instance, if you expect your audience to have software that's similar to yours and be at about your level of computer literacy, then you'll be free to include just about anything you have access to on your own computer. But if you plan to create a Web page that can be read by just about anyone regardless of their computer competency, hardware, or software, you'll have to consider the possibility that some people will only have access to a text-based Internet browser such as Lynx. A potential viewer may be using an older slow-speed modem that is makes it impossible to view your graphics and buttons. This means you will have to provide for text-alternatives. You'll need to include linked text alongside link icons and buttons.

Margaret Riley recommends keeping your text file as small as possible and never more than 50K. Likewise, limit your graphics in size and complexity, perhaps not more than 25K. Otherwise, your reader may grow old waiting for your home page artistry to download to his or her screen.

Storing Portfolio Items

With the audience rooted firmly in mind, create a working folder to store items for your on-line portfolio. Fill the folder with scanned images of artifacts, documents, 3-D images, sound tracks, actual letters of reference, and software samples. Then establish a separate Web folder for your Web site documents. This folder begins with the actual home page in HTML code and must contain all documents that will ultimately be linked to this page. Typically, you'll be moving items from the working folder to your Web folder.

After collecting and creating your samples, you will have to consider final selection and sequence. Since this is a visual medium, you might want to use a storyboard outline for planning the overall organization. Some people may choose the tried-and-true method of creating index cards to represent pages and hyperlinked documents. I find it helpful to create a dummy hard copy first as a model for my screen version.

ORGANIZING YOUR PORTFOLIO WEB PAGES

As discussed in chapter 10, there are three general methods for organizing the contents of printed portfolios: chronological, functional, and thematic. With a hyperlinked Web page, you have the added possibility of letting the reader browse your document in a nonlinear fashion, selecting what interests him or her and randomly viewing different artifacts with the click of a button. However, in the interest of simplicity, I recommend a linear approach, because people are still most comfortable with scrolling down the screen rather than jumping all over.

For instance, after viewing a succinct and attractive home page, the reader scrolls to a section titled *Sample of Strategic Planning*. The second screen fills with a short summary of the documents linked to this page, such as lists of organizations you advise, a sample table of contents from a strategic plan, a report from an evaluation team, etc. After reading about these samples, the reader has the option of moving on to pages (screens) where these actual items can be viewed and then clicking on hot buttons or hypertext links that will take him or her back to the previous page or the home page.

In sum, keep visual simplicity, consistency, and unity in mind as you create your electronic portfolio. Think in terms of a person quickly scanning your home page. They need an enticing summary with hypertext links pointing to supporting documents. These hot links must come alive and invite exploration. Unlike the conventional résumé that organizes the paper page around fairly staid headings such as *Education, Work Experience,* and *Awards,* I suggest being a bit more descriptive. For instance, try writing text links that draw the reader into what lies behind them. Instead of labeling a hot link with the word *Education,* try the phrase *Samples of Scholastic Excellence.* Clicking on these words takes the reader to lists of outstanding grades in key courses, references from teachers, or lists of scholarships and awards. Another hot link might read *Samples of Effective Leadership and Communication.* Click here and a video clip shows the job seeker accepting an award on behalf of a service club.

Headers, Titles, E-mail

As you begin designing your final Web page, carefully consider the title, which only shows at the top of the screen. When people search the Internet, they hunt for key words using various search engines. Your title fuels these search engines, and keeping it brief and informative makes finding you easier. Your title could be picked by people and organizations compiling lists of new Web sites on the Internet, or end up as a bookmark in an individual's Internet address book. (A bookmark stores your Web address for future use when Web surfing). Therefore, the job-search portfolio title should include a unique name or your area of expertise (both if possible). Conduct a search for key words that might be used in your title. This might tell you if a search engine will be able to find your page and then display it within the first three screens of a search summary.

You'll also want to make sure that the information a browser lists about your page will be clear and entice the reader to actually select your Web site for reading. For additional ideas, consider Jack Chapman's title suggestions on Special Reports in chapter 10. He is a master at creating brief and succinct titles and urges people to use a title that makes clear the benefits to the reader. For instance, if your experience includes saving on health insurance costs, you might want to title your portfolio Web page *Reducing Health Costs.* Maybe the president will e-mail you!

If your browser supports the creation of forms, you'll also want to use it to make it simple for people to contact you by including the option for e-mailing from your Web page. When the viewer clicks on this button, an e-mail window form appears, addressed to you. It's like including an automated return envelope. The sheer simplicity encourages interaction. If your design is for everyone, including people who may not be able to use this feature, then also prominently display your e-mail address.

The Final Test

Since you can never be sure how your page will look to others, the final stage of development involves testing before publishing or distributing it on the Web. Begin with your own computer. Try changing the size of the window to see if the page stays intact. Test all the hot buttons or hypertext link to make sure everything comes up as planned. Put your home page and associated files on a disk and try them out on computers using different hardware and software. Finally, send your portfolio over the wire (or by disk) for others to field-test for you. You may need to include the browser or viewer software associated with your home page (assuming the creator grants you permission to distribute it freely).

NETWORKING ON THE NET

Like face-to-face networking, networking on the Internet takes time, and the results depend on the quality of your interaction. If you try to randomly advertise your Web page on a Listserv or Newsgroup without first learning about the members and contributing to their ongoing discussion, your announcement will appear self-serving and ultimately become counterproductive.

Begin as a silent spectator, observing the dialogue in a given Newsgroup or Listserv. Subscribe and just listen to the dialogue for awhile. During this get-acquainted time, you'll develop a sensitivity for the language, interests, and expertise of the particular group. You'll soon be able to pick out the blowhards as well as the thoughtful and informed individuals. When you feel you understand the environment of your cyberspace niche, begin making contact; contribute to the discussion by posting a message to everyone or mailing it just to selected individuals.

If you have written or collected useful information that might be of interest to the entire group, offer to share. If you have read an interesting article in your profession, summarize and ask for feedback. Others might post a typical problem faced at work and ask others for advice. For instance, someone who was asked by her manager to downsize her staff from two members to one might describe the size of her operation and ask other people in her on-line group how many staffers they had in their offices. She could use this on-line survey to support her position in the next meeting with the budget cutters in her office. Other people share quotes and jokes to bring a bit of lightness to the discussion. In this manner, you gradually cultivate meaningful relationships with people you will probably never meet. As you elevate yourself from on-line spectator to active member, you'll earn the privilege of contacting your on-line community any time you need assistance.

How do you find an electronic community in which you can feel in synch with members?

Networking Techniques

Start by identifying groups that share your interests. Find a group discussing topics related to your profession, employment status, or even your personal interests. You can use Internet searching software such as Lycos, WebCrawler, Alta Vista, and Veronica. You can collect e-mail, Web site, and Internet resource addresses from computer magazines, newspaper columns, and professional journals, as well as on-line magazines and discussion groups. As you review the contents of a bulletin board, copy down the names and comments of people who might share a common passion.

Next, write to these people individually on-line and introduce yourself. You can begin by mentioning things you have in common, asking questions, or offering to share something that might interest them. As the relationship grows, you can begin to ask if they might have information or advice that could help you in your job search. Perhaps they'd be willing to look at your résumé or portfolio and offer feedback. This is the electronic version of informational interviewing.

You can turn yourself into an Internet magnet and attract total strangers when you upload a useful resource. Some people compile lists of useful contacts and helpful Internet sites. Several individuals write monthly newsletters summing up trends in their industry. Others create reports, how-to documents, or tip sheets pertaining to specific techniques. Still, others offer to mail informative products from their workplace. You could make a list of upcoming conferences and training events based on the newsletters you receive.

I have often uploaded, posted, and e-mailed excerpts from books, new recipes, poems, jokes, and essays. In less than two years, I've built an Internet Rolodex of 250+ names from across the country and around the world. Most of the contributors in the book you're now reading found my document about portfolios first and then e-mailed me. As a result, most of my research for this book was done from my keyboard; it was great fun reading people rather than books. Sharing is the key to prospecting or researching on-line, just as it is in the real world. (Except in the real world, it takes much longer!)

You might choose to conclude each item you upload with a brief biographical profile, listing your profession, e-mail address, and, if you wish, a request for information. The ending profile in one of my documents reads: "Biographical Profile—Martin Kimeldorf is a teacher and author. I am currently looking for information about how people use portfolios. If you have any useful information or know of someone who might, I would appreciate hearing from you. You can contact me at MKportf@aol.com."

Remember this golden Internet rule: The Net is an information nexus; people who offer to share useful information become known.

Margaret F. Riley offers another suggestion for getting known. Try to register your new portfolio Web page with the various search engines and indexers such as Lycos, WebCrawler, and Alta Vista. You can e-mail the Webmaster for details about submission. And finally, consult books that list on-line résumé services, recruiters, and employment services. Try to post a résumé with them and include your Web site address. On your Web site, be sure to include a text copy of your résumé so it can be easily downloaded and saved into a database by an interested employer.

Finally, don't forget the most widespread media of all—print. Put your e-mail and Web page address on résumés, business cards, and stationery. Include your home page URL address at the end of your e-mail. In addition, notify people in your personal and cyberspace network.

How to Frame Your Request for Assistance
Review all the postings and write down the names and addresses of anyone who might appear to have something in common with your profession or job-search

Is Your Budget or Time Limited?

Not everyone has unlimited access to the Internet. Or you may have just received a pink slip, which has sent you into a dead panic, and you don't feel you have the luxury of time to build a set of quality contacts. As an intermediate step, begin visiting electronic bulletin boards found on local on-line networks or at sites devoted to employment in a particular state or profession. You can even get free access to these sites by using computers equipped with modems, found in many public libraries.

goals. Then e-mail this list of possible contacts a short, standard, but individually addressed message. Refer to their postings and end by asking for advice. The trick is not to ask for specific advice about openings because this plea may sound very blunt to a total stranger. Don't ask "Do you have information about hospitality jobs in Kentucky?" but, instead, ask for advice about where you could get information: "Do you know anyone who might have information about the hospitality profession in Kentucky? I am thinking about moving there soon, and I am looking for contacts who might know what's going on in the field there."

I once used this approach when trying to figure out where to submit my new cookbook. I knew that cookbooks were very hard to sell, so I tried networking on a commercial network with anyone who had included the words *cook* and *writing* in their on-line profile. I found over 200 entries and sent mail to about fifty people. I got back several helpful replies and the names of three editors in publishing houses.

Where to Get Started

After logging on, it's easy to get overwhelmed by the huge reservoir of information sitting on the other side of your modem. Fortunately, some people and organizations have collected information or provided tools for finding the information you need about careers. One of the best places to visit first is Riley's Job Guide (http://www.jobtrak.com/jobguide/). This site offers loads of practical information, and the author has reviewed and selected the finest sites in the career field, which you can access through links on her site. If you need a general search tool for career information or information related to your area of expertise, then the general-purpose search engine and index created at Yahoo (http://www.yahoo.com) is a good place to begin. In addition to these great starting points, you might find the following list useful as you begin to zero in on your specific career information needs:

General Career Support
Career Magazine   http://www.careermag.com
Career Mosaic   http://www.careermosaic.com

Job Center   http://www.jobcenter.com
Monster Board and On-line Job Center   http://www.monster.com

Want Ads and Company Information Specialty
E-Span (want ads)   http://www.espan.com
America's Job Bank (job service listings)   http://www.ajb.dni.us/
Hoovers On-line (company information)   http://www.hoovers.com
Virtual Job Fair   http://www.careerexpo.com/vjf.html

College-Oriented Opportunities for Grads
JobWeb (set up by a college consortium)   http://www.jobweb.org
Union College CDC   http://apollo.union.edu/CDC/CRH.HO.html

Executives and Managers
Exec-U-Net   http://www.clickit.com/touch/execunet/execunet.htm
TOP jobs-USA   http://www.fiber.net

Specialized Samples
JobTailor (portfolio model)   http://www.jobtailor.com/
City.Net (for long distance search)   http:///www.city.net.
Seattle Times (sample newspaper)   http://www.seatimes.com
Washington's State Employment Resources   http://www.wa.gov/employ.html
Match your personality to your career path   http://www.hawk.igs.net/careers

CONCLUSION

Nearer to the Heart's Desire

Ah, Love!
Could you and I with Him conspire
To grasp this sorry Scheme of Things entire,
Would not we shatter it to bits—and then
Re-mold it nearer to the Heart's Desire!
                            —Omar Khayyam, *The Rubaiyat*

▶ In the last part of the twentieth century, we find ourselves searching for personal prosperity in a land where abundance is giving way to scarcity. On this road to self-improvement, we have been inundated with advice-giving and how-to books. "Experts" study successful people and then advise us how to mimic them. They stand before the podium and urge us to visualize an outcome, make five-year plans. Others celebrate the serendipitous quality of life. They tell us to embrace change and the unknown. Don't worry, take a leap, the net will appear.

Neither group's message rings true for me. The only thing I have consistently and successfully planned for is my weekly food shopping list. Unfortunately, work opportunities being offered today shift so frequently that effective long-term planning is just about impossible. And embracing the unknown is like hugging an ice cube—the harder I try to hold it, the quicker it melts away.

You and I both know that the task at hand is to mold the very best life out of the clay we've been given. We can wish for luck, but we cannot plan on it. Our challenge is to discover new opportunities with the least amount of risk.

I believe all of us have been granted some choice in the part we play in this life and the lines we speak. Each of us enters the stage with a purpose, but it isn't always clear at first, and sometimes, it takes a lifetime to reveal. For me, the key is to become more aware of who I am and where I'd like to go. I have found that chronicling my lifework in a portfolio prompts me into a more aware state. I use my portfolio to help define the character I'd like to play. In the darkness of the theater, I hang onto my hopes, and I keep my eyes wide open. And after reviewing the pages of my portfolio, I dream upon the blank pages yet to fill, and I see many more possibilities than I first imagined.

As you fill the pages of your portfolio, I hope it fills you with a new sense of your potentialities. Perhaps, as a result, you will be more prepared to remold the next scene of your life a bit closer to your heart's desire.

APPENDIX A

Suggestions for Personal Portfolios

This is a list of commonly collected personal items. Look it over for ideas about things you might collect now or wish to start collecting in the future for a personal portfolio.

Album covers
Antiques
Artwork
Athletic letters, memorabilia
Autographs
Awards, ribbons, plaques, or certificates
Books and manuscripts
Bottle caps, glasses, or bottles
Brochures
Bumper stickers
Buttons, bumper stickers, pins with slogans
Cartoons
Celebrity items (autographs, gossip, etc.)
Certificates (birth, death, marriage, divorce)
China, glassware, demitasse sets
Clocks, watches, time pieces
Coins or stamps
Computer software or works
Decals
Dolls
Financial documents (IRS, budgets, stubs)
Hats
Handmade crafts or items
Insects
Jewelry
Journals or diaries
Keys
Letters, e-mail, memos
License plates
Lists
Magazines or newspapers or articles
Maps
Masks
Matchbooks

Membership cards (clubs, unions, organizations)
Mementos, souvenirs
Menus
Miniatures or models
Music
Music or records
Natural objects (rocks, shells, flowers, butterflies)
Notes
Objects I made
Objects from friendship, peace, or volunteering
Photos
Poetry
Political campaign materials
Postcards or travel mementos
Programs, flyers
Puzzles
Quotations
Recipes
Religious objects
Research papers
Résumés
School-related items (report cards, old school papers, yearbooks)
Seeds
Stuffed or wind-up animals
Swap-ables (garage sales, swap meets, flea market)
Tapestries
Tests or scores
Thank-you notes
Ticket stubs
Trading cards
Videotapes, home movies

APPENDIX B

Suggestions for Professional Portfolios

This is a starter list illustrating some of the work samples that could be included in a professional portfolio. Look it over for ideas about things you might collect now or wish to start collecting in the future. Appendix C contains related work-world words that can be used in captions. Reviewing that list might also fire up neurons in the career segment of your brain.

Career Explorations Documents (for students and people with limited work experience)

Compile this kind of "preemployment" evidence when you have limited experience in your chosen field or most of your experiences come from school. These artifacts establish the fact that you possess a work ethic and work maturity.

Goal-Setting Documents

- Notes from career research or informational interviews
- Results from a career interest test showing your interests aligned with work sought
- Results from a vocational aptitude test that establish a talent base for the work sought
- Commendations or evaluations from student work-study programs such as campus jobs, internships, co-op work, summer jobs, service learning projects
- Samples of academic excellence illustrating the capacity for hard work and independent learning (graded work from teachers)
- Professional testing results, such as NTE, PPST, FE, GRE Subject Test results

Formal and Informal Education or Training

- Brochures describing training events, retreats, workshops, clinics, lecture series
- Certificate of mastery or completion
- Charts or lists showing hours or time completed in various areas of study
- Evidence of participation in vocational competitions
- Grants, loans, scholarships secured for schooling
- Licenses and certifications
- Lists of competencies mastered
- Samples from classes (papers, projects, reports, displays, video or computer samples)
- Samples from personal studies (notes, binders, products)
- Syllabi or course descriptions for classes and workshops
- Standardized or formalized tests
- Teacher evaluations
- Transcripts, report cards

General Work Performance

- Attendance records
- Community service projects
- Descriptive material about the organization (annual report, brochure, newsletters, articles)
- Job description

- Logs, lists, or charts showing general effort (phone calls received, extra hours worked, overtime, volume of e-mail, case load, transactions completed, sales volumes)
- Military records, awards, badges
- Employer evaluations or reviews
- Examples of problem solving
- Letters of reference
- List of clients you assisted
- Organization charts showing personnel, procedures, or resources
- Printouts of e-mail, Web pages, journals, memos, articles that mention your efforts
- Products showing your leadership qualities (mission statements, agendas, networks)
- Records showing how your students, clients, or patients did after receiving your services (evidence showing your impact on the lives and performances of others such as test scores, performance improvement data, or employment and promotion)
- Résumés
- Samples from (or lists showing) participation in professional organizations, committees, work teams
- Surveys showing satisfaction by customers, clients, students, patients, etc.
- Invitations to share your expertise (letters or agreements asking you to train, mentor, or counsel others; invitations to present at conferences or professional gatherings)
- Documentation of experience as a consultant (letters requesting your services, products, proposals)
- Letters of commendation, thank-you letters, letters of nomination

Work Samples Illustrating Specific or Specialized Skills

Data
- Communication pieces (memos, reports, P.R. documents, a public service announcement)

- Writing abilities as demonstrated in actual samples of your writing (articles, proposals, scripts, training materials, editing sheet)
- Evidence of public speaking (membership in Toastmasters International, photograph of you at podium, speech outline, brochure for your presentation, speaker's badge or brochure, blurb from the conference); posters, photos, reviews of actual performances (dance, drama, music, storytelling)
- Data (graphs, charts, tables you helped to produce, testing results)
- Display or performance materials (actual objects, illustrations, or posters from displays)
- Computer-related information (database designed, desktop publishing documents, samples from Internet surfing and Web pages, computer video screen pictures, or manual covers illustrating programs you use)
- Formal and technical documents as in grant or loan applications (include proposal cover sheet or award letter), technical manual
- Evidence of research skills (publications, charts, slides, papers, awards)

People
- People and leadership skills (projects or committees you chair, projects you initiated, photos of you with important people, mentoring programs, proposals, documents or strategies related to negotiation)
- Evidence of your ability to plan, coordinate, or manage time, people, and materials (procedure sheets, policy statements, schedules, itineraries, planning documents)
- Instruments used to gather information and input (such as surveys or focus group)
- Problem solving illustrated with various artifacts (use figures or pictures showing improvements in products, services, prof-

its, safety, quality, or time; include forms and other paper products used to solve problems)
- Employee training packets, interview sheets, motivational activities
- Short stories or lists that illustrate your executive or management skills (e.g., futures-oriented, an entrepreneurial spirit, mediation talents, employee empowerment, total quality approaches)

Things
(any artifact that shows a technical skill, equipment, or specialized procedures used in your work)

- Paper documents or replicas of actual items, including forms, charts, printouts (such as medical chart, financial statement or budgets, reports, emergency preparedness plan, marketing plan, customer satisfaction plan, inspection or evaluation sheet, financial or budget plans, spreadsheets, charts, official documents)
- Performance records (keyboard timing scores; safety records; phone logs; complaint logs; pay stub with hours worked highlighted and other data deleted; any record showing volume, amount, total time, response time, turnaround time, dollars or sales figures, size of customer database; organization chart showing people supervised)
- Technical directions, manuals, procedure sheets for specialized work, use of equipment, and detailed processes; this could include sample pages from manuals, illustrations, technical drawings, blueprints or schematics, photos from the workplace, schematics or directions for tools or equipment, operation or procedure sheet
- Photos, video, slide show, or multimedia presentation showing process or equipment
- Actual item that can be handled in various ways—displayed in person one at a time or part of a display you set up

- Displays, art work, exhibits, bulletin boards

Military Artifacts Demonstrating Expertise, Training, and Employability

The forms, transcripts, reports, awards, and commendations listed next can testify to your employability, training, and scholastic abilities. However, you will need to use portfolio captions, section summaries, and introductory text to highlight the relevant information and explain the implications to a civilian employer or college.

- VMET (Verification of Military Education)
- DD Form 214—Certificate of Release or Discharge From Active Duty
- Personnel qualifications records known as DA 2A (for enlisted soldiers) and DA 2B (for officers)
- DLPT—Defense Language Proficiency Test
- Security clearance notification
- Certificates (verifying competence in various areas such as driving trucks, parachuting, preparing prescription drugs, working in air traffic control)
- Evaluation reports (Officer Evaluation Report, Non-Commissioned Officer Evaluation Report and Counseling Statements for enlisted soldiers)
- Academic evaluation report
- Commendations and awards (plus the written justification for the award or commendation)
- Logs that demonstrate a level of performance or experience such as flight logs, training logs, repair logs, mileage logs, and access logs
- Training Certificates (plus your competitive standing describing where you placed such as the top 10 percent of the class, first place finisher, etc.)

Skill Words

Here I've grouped conventional skill words into three lists: skills of *Data, People,* and *Things.* You may want to concentrate on the one or two of the groups that most closely reflect your interests, but don't neglect the rest because many words such as "polished" could have been placed in more than one category such as "polishing one's writing" or "polishing metal and stones."

Data

(skills used in comparing, compiling, distributing, writing, speaking, analyzing, presenting, computing, or coordinating information)

accounted
advertised
analyzed
analyzed figures
articulated
assigned
audited
authored
authorized
budgeted
calculated
charted
clarified
classified
collected
communicated
compared
composed
computed
condensed
consolidated
contacted
contracted
controlled
coordinated
corresponded
debated
debugged
defined
designed
diagnosed
displayed
distributed
drafted
dramatized
edited
enforced
enhanced
entered
estimated
evaluated
expressed
faxed
field-tested
filed
financed
interpreted
inventoried
investigated
judged
logged
measured
organized
polished
predicted
presented
printed
promoted

published
purchased
quantified
queried
questioned
recommended
researched
responded
reviewed
routed
scheduled
solicited
sorted
standardized
studied
systematized
summarized
supervised
synthesized
tabulated
telephoned
terminated
translated
transmitted
typed

People and Animals

(skills used in serving, caring for teaching, supervising, communicating, persuading, or monitoring)

accompanied
administered
advised
advocated
allocated
appointed
approved
arbitrated
arranged
assisted
awarded
cared for
chaired
coached
communicated
consulted
convinced
coordinated
counseled

decided
demonstrated
directed
disciplined
discussed
elected
employed
entertained
escorted
explained
explored
facilitated
guided
hired
hosted
influenced
instructed
interviewed
inventoried
judged
lectured
led
listened
lobbied
managed
mentored
monitored
motivated
negotiated
networked
nursed
oriented
performed
persuaded
piloted
pioneered
planned
presented
prioritized
promoted
protected
recommended
recruited
rehabilitated
reinforced
resolved
set goals
studied
supervised
supported

surveyed
taught
tested
trained
transported
tutored
umpired
visited

Things and Plants
(skills related to using equipment, machines, tools, materials, hands-on or laboring, crafting, creating, performing)

adapted
accelerated
arranged
assembled
assured quality
butchered
calibrated
cleansed
compared
composed
constructed
cooked
delivered
designed
diagnosed
enameled
evaluated
experimented
explored
fabricated
fastened
forged
harmonized
harvested
heat-treated
identified
illustrated
improved standards

inspected
installed
invented
inventoried
laminated
launched
maintained
measured
minimized risk
modeled
operated
operated
overhauled
oversaw
packaged
patented
performed
photographed
plotted
printed
programmed
recorded
refined
regulated
rehabilitated
reinforced
remodeled
renewed
repaired
rescued
restored
routed
setup
signaled
sized
sketched
tended
tested
tuned
upgraded
welded

APPENDIX D

Personality Words Describing Temperament, Self-Management, and Interpersonal Skills

These words describe personal style, the way one goes about doing things. You will find words here that describe how you work with people, show responsibility, manage or discipline yourself, and factors related to integrity.

Teamwork and People Skills

adaptable
broad- or open-minded
cooperative
courteous and considerate
democratic
expresses ideas clearly
fair minded
flexible
friendly or warm
good listener
participates on committees or work-teams
sensitive
sensitive to diversified population
solves problems within a group
tactful or diplomatic

Responsibility Indicators

accurate
attend to details
careful
conscientious
deliberate
follows directions
manage time well
mature
meets deadlines
methodical
precise
punctual
reliable
serious

steady
trustworthy

Work Habits

competitive
efficient
energetic
entrepreneurial
hard-working
independent
industrious
manage goals
motivated
persevering
persistent
quick
saver—of time or money
self-starter
tenacious
work without supervision, self-directed

Intellectual Traits

creative
curious
eager to learn
expands knowledge base
imaginative
innovative
inventive
logical
problem-solving attitude
reflective

resourceful
self-learner
welcomes new challenges

Personal Qualities

adventurous, courageous
assertive
balanced values
businesslike
confident
demonstrates self-control
enthusiastic, cheerful

fair, honest, ethical
good-natured, optimistic
handles pressure or stress
healthy lifestyle
idealistic
loyal
patient
practical
sense of humor
sensible
takes pride in appearance
tough-minded

RESOURCES

Portfolio Books and Resources

Authoring Your Days In Journals And Personal Portfolios by Martin Kimeldorf. If you enjoy compiling a journal and would like to apply your portfolio skills to areas outside of work, then you'll enjoy this book. It includes techniques for personal journals as well as personal portfolios. The background information, examples, and exercises are designed to stimulate your creative juices and provide guidance in assessing where you've been and want to go in life. As you examine your interests, passions, challenges, and significant life transitions, you'll develop a deeper understanding of the patterns that make you unique. This work-in-progress is available to the readers of this book.

The Advertising Portfolio, Creating an Effective Presentation of Your Work by Ann Marie Barry. NTC Business Book, Lincolnwood, IL, 1990.

Creating Portfolios For Success in School, Work, and Life by Martin Kimeldorf. Free Spirit Press Inc., Minneapolis, MN, 1994. The student workbook and teacher guide is written for young adults who are typically creating portfolios as part of a school experience.

Help Wanted, An Inexperienced Job Seeker's Complete Guide To Career Success by Ann M. Gill and Stephen M. Lewis. Waveland Press, Prospect Heights, IL, 1996. This book contains an excellent chapter on portfolios.

How To Prepare Your Portfolio by Ed Marquand. New York: Art Direction Book Company, 1994. This book was originally written for students and artists and while it emphasizes art portfolios, it contains useful information about different materials available from traditional leather portfolios and paper stocks to plastic holding devices and computer diskettes. It also includes many good tips about organization and assembly.

Life Work Portfolio. National Occupational Information Coordinating Committee (NOICC), Washington, DC, 1996. This product includes a process and place (envelopes) for developing your actual portfolio. There is a proven career development sequence for creating a holistic plan for your lifework. After developing a career path in your portfolio, the book takes you to the next steps in planning for education or job finding.

Portfolio Development Handbook, Prior Learning Experience Program by Peter Omar Manuelian. City University, Bellevue, WA, 1991. Available in the college bookstore (tel. 800-426-5596).

Portfolio Development Independent Study Guide by Roberta Burke. PLA Office, Mohawk College of Applied Arts & Technology, P.O. Box 2034, Hamilton, Ontario L8N 3T2, 1994. This curriculum has been widely used in Canada as part of Prior Learning Assessment programs where students can receive credit based on submitting a portfolio documenting prior learning experiences.

Portfolio Portraits by Donald H. Graves and Bonnie S. Sunstein, eds. Heinemann, Portsmouth, NH, 1992. This is an excellent background book examining the practice and potential of using résumés as a teaching and learning medium.

The Teaching Portfolio: A Practical Guide to Improved Performance and Promotion/ Tenure by Peter Seldin. Anker Publishing Company Inc., Boston, MA, 1991.

Tour of Duty Chronicle by Army Times Publishing Co., Springfield, VA (tel. 800-368-5718). This scrapbook is designed for activity duty, separated, or retired military members. The binder sized at 18.5 by 13.5 inches can hold twenty clear vinyl pocket pages that allow you to hold odd-size and over-size items such as certificates, diplomas, awards, and other memorabilia. Different versions are designed for each branch of the service.

Sample Design Books

The Aldus Guide To Basic Design by Roger C. Parker. Aldus Corp. Seattle, WA, 1987. Typical of the books written that emphasize design.

Editing By Design by Jan V. White. R. R. Bowker Co., New York, NY, 1982. This is a classic in the field of design and an excellent starting point for increasing your design literacy.

Looking Good In Print by Roger C. Parker. Ventana Press, Inc. Chapel Hill, NC, 1988. One of my favorite books because it is short and well illustrated. Though Aldus has merged with another company, you can contact the current makers of Pagemaker software and inquire about this or similar books.

Books About the Changing Way We Do Work

The Age Of Unreason by Charles Handy. Harvard Business School Press, 1990. The book catalogs how people will lead "portfolio" lives. People's lives and work become a collection of different temporary assignments and relationships rather than long-term routines.

The End of Work: The Decline of the Global Labor Force and the Dawn of the Post-Market Era by Jeremy Rifkin. Jeremy P. Tarcher/Putnam. New York, NY, 1994.

Job Shift, How To Prosper In A Workplace Without Jobs by William Bridges. Addison-Wesley Publishing Co. Reading, MA, 1994.

General Career and Job-Search Books

Beating Job Burnout by Paul Stevens. VGM Career Horizons, Lincolnwold, IL, 1995. Written by one of Australia's leading authorities on career development, this book sets out a process for identifying your passions and interests. He then guides you in making meaningful career transitions or suggests ways to enrich the totality of your "worklife."

Damn Good Résumé (books, guides, software, newsletters) by Yana Parker. Ten Speed Press. Berkeley, CA. Yana writes for both the job seeker and the professional résumé writer. She provides a wide range of materials with a wide range of résumé samples (blue collar to navy blue suit).

Does Your Résumé Wear Combat Boots by William G. Fitzpatrick and C. Edward Good. Prima Publishing, Rocklin, CA, 1993. Anyone separating from the service will find this easy-to-follow book very helpful.

Educator's Job Search by Martin Kimeldorf. National Education Association, Washington, DC, 1994.

Guerrilla Tactics in the New Job Market (2nd ed.) by Tom Jackson. Bantam Books, New York, NY. A popular book containing insider advice to help you get past the hurdles and the "no's."

How to Make $1000 a Minute Negotiating Your Salaries and Raises by Jack Chapman. Ten Speed Press, Berkeley, CA, 1987. To get a copy of his Special Report, write and ask for "Amazing New Job-Search Tool . . ." at 511 Maple Ave, Wilmette, IL 60091.

How NOT To Make It . . . And Succeed: Life On Your Own Terms by Anna Miller-Tiedeman, Ph.D. Upper Access, 1989 (tel. 800-356-9315). This book explodes the notion that career is something "out there" in your future, to be chosen, planned, pursued, and reached. Instead, the author talks in terms of a career as here-and-now.

Imagine Loving Your Work by Marti Chaney with Vicki Thayer. Celestial Arts, Berkeley, CA, 1993. A good process approach to career change and entrance, especially geared for women. The authors also recommend portfolios to the reader.

Job Search Networking by Richard Beatty. Bob Adams Inc., Holbrook, MA, 1994. The subtitle of the book says it all: "Learn How More than 68 Percent of All Jobs are Found." This is a very practical and useful resource on what are considered the most powerful job-hunting tactics around.

Marketing Yourself for a Second Career by Col. Doug Carter, USAGE-Ret. Retired Officer's Association, Alexandria, VA, 1989. This is an excellent and well-written resource for people making the transition from the military to civilian jobs.

Out of Uniform: Guide to Military Transition to Civilian Employment by Harry Drier. Career, Education and Training Associates, Inc., 1236 Langston Drive, Columbus, OH 43220, 1994. This work has been extremely well-received by military personnel including those in the Reserves and National Guard.

What Color Is Your Parachute? by Dick Bolles. Ten Speed Press, Berkeley, CA, 1995. Annually revised, this work has kept hope alive for twenty-five-plus years. It deals with all dimensions of one's career and contains excellent material about informational interviewing.

VGM's Guide to Temporary Employment by Lewis R. Baratz. VGM Career Horizons, Lincolnwood, IL, 1995. For those who want to make the most of temporary work, this book offers many helpful insights as well as an honest appraisal of the blessings and pitfalls.

Electronic Job Search and Education Tools

Electronic Résumé Revolution, Electronic Résumé Revolution, and *Hook Up, Get Hired* by Joyce Lain Kennedy. John Wiley and Sons Inc., New York, NY, 1994 and 1995. This triumvirate of digital virtuosity is must reading for anyone thinking about computers, job seeking, and the future. They contain bushels of techniques and background, written in an easy-to-follow style.

The Internet University-Courses By Computer by Dan Corrigan. Cape Software, Harwich, MA, 1996. Written in the style of a computer manual but with many examples and down-to-earth style, this is the definitive work about lifelong learning on-line. Topics and lists include accredited colleges offering courses and degrees from GEDs to Ph.D.s, adult education, financial aid and scholarships, course descriptions, and essays by leaders in this field. The book material can be updated via Website (http://www.caso.com/).

The PLA Guide To Internet Job Searching by Margaret F. Riley. VGM Career Horizons, Lincolnwood, IL, 1996. A helpful guide to using the Internet's resources and networks in your job search. There are hundreds of resources listed, each with an evaluation of its major features. Written by a well-respected Internet expert on behalf of the Public Library Association (PLA).

Occupational and Career References, Resources, Tests, Services

Career Change: Everything You Need To Know To Meet New Challenges And Take Control Of Your Career by Dr. David P. Helfand. This book provides valuable background about the major occupational guidance materials available.

Career Success Workbook by Urban G. Whitaker. The Learning Center, San Francisco, CA, 1992. Whitaker's books have helped many people in career transition. His pamphlet and book are designed to help the reader bridge the gap between transferable skills and education preparation.

Self Directed Search by John Holland. PAR, Odessa, FL, 1994. This easy to administer career test provides feedback about careers that match your temperament, values, and interests. The resulting list of jobs contain RIASEC codes that are matched to various books describing different occupations. Different tests target various age groups.

The Complete Guide for Occupational Exploration (CGOE), The Guide for Occupational Exploration (GOE), The Enhanced Guide for Occupational Exploration (EGOE), and *Occupational Outlook Handbook (OOH)*. These reference titles were formerly printed by the U.S. Government and now are available through JIST Works Inc., Indianapolis, IN. JIST also combines several versions of these resources on a single CD-ROM disk and computers disks for PCs.

Invitation to Portfolio Power, Part II

This book, and others like it, are only the beginning of the portfolio story. As you adapt the portfolio to your specific personal and professional needs, you become a contributor to this story, shaping how professional portfolios are created and how they will be used. As I emphasized in the introduction, there is no "right way to do it." Consider this book as only a starting point. In fact, I'm certain that you'll probably invent some new approaches along the way. Once you've completed this book you'll be a colleague, and I invite you to submit your ideas and insights, samples or perhaps entire portfolio for consideration for Portfolio Power, Part II. The power of learning from models is well known, and I envision this new book as a compilation of models—stories and samples from people like you.

Guidelines for Submitting Material for Portfolio Power, Part II

If you'd like to share samples, entire portfolios, stories, or insights from your personal or professional portfolios, please e-mail me first at MKportf@aol.com to get the guidelines. Write up a description of what you'd like to have considered for inclusion and limit the description to a single page. Do not send any documents, portfolios, or samples; unfortunately, I will not be able to return any that I receive.

Martin Kimeldorf
January 1997

INDEX

A

Accomplishments
    in career portfolio, 41–42
    in lifework database, 43, 48
    military, 87–95
    in professional portfolio, 11–16
The Advertising Portfolio, 106, 179
The Age of Unreason, 32, 180
The Aldus Guide to Basic Design, 180
Anxiety, in presenting portfolio, 68–69
Archiving
    for career portfolio, 35
    for personal portfolio, 26–29
Arter, Judith, 4
Artifacts, 99–103
    analyzed using occupational codes, 53–54
    for career portfolio, 35
    cataloging, 28–29
    claiming greatness by association, 102–3
    commonplace, telling story behind, 99–100
    connected to existing job options, 50–53
    connected to skills and outcomes, 44
    examples, 44–45
    in lifework database, 46
    military, 93
    for personal portfolio, 22–26
    symbolic, crafting, 100–102
Assets (professional) management. *See*
    Lifelong learning portfolio
Audience for portfolio, 105, 106
    analyzing, 108–9, 141
*Authoring Your Days in Journals and Personal
    Portfolios,* 179

B

Baratz, Lewis R., 181
Barry, Ann Marie, 106, 179
Beam, David, 77
Beating Job Burnout, 180
Beatty, Richard, 181
Beginning portfolio. *See* Starting portfolio
Bolles, Richard, 55, 181
Book Blitz, 68
Books and guides, 179–82
Bridges, William, 32, 180
Burke, Roberta, 179

Business marketing portfolio, 69–71

C

Captions. *See* Content and captions
Career advancement portfolio, 73–78
    employee evaluation procedures and, 75–78
    preparing for lateral changes, 74–75
    preparing for promotions and evaluations,
        73–74
Career portfolios
    analyzing artifacts using occupational
        codes, 53–54
    archiving for, 35
    conceptualizing new possibilities, 49
    connecting artifacts to existing job options,
        50–53
    connecting artifacts to skills and outcomes,
        44–47
    contemporary and future value of, 32–33
    crafting, 35–36
    digital frontier in occupational information
        systems, 56
    exercises, 38–42, 44, 47–49, 53–54
    expanded view of self, 42–43
    feedback on, 57
    lifework database, 38–39
    occupational references, 51–55
    reality testing and adapting ideal job titles,
        50
    skill–factoring for, 36–38
    as skills catalog, 33–34
    skills identification, 39–42
    starting assembly of, 31–32
    taken on informational interviews, 55, 57
    thematic view of work, 47–48
Careers. *See also* Job *and* Work *entries*
    portfolios and, 12
    resources, 180–82
Career Success Workbook, 182
Carter, Col. Doug, 181
Cataloging artifacts, 28–29
CGOE, 54, 89, 182
Chaney, Marti, 47, 181
Chapman, Jack, 117, 120, 121–22, 159, 181
Chronological organization, 113, 115, 116
Churn, reducing, 101

Closing reflection, 135–36
Collecting information, 26–28
College career placement centers, 86
Communication. *See also* Design of portfolio;
    Job search portfolio
    content and captions, 105–12
    crafting artifacts, 99–103
    electronic, 147–63
    in interviews, 64
    of military skills and accomplishments,
      91–93
    presentation of portfolio, 65–69
Compensation, performance reviews and,
    73–78
Competition, 12
The Complete Guide for Occupational
    Exploration, 54, 89, 182
Components of portfolio, 3, 12
    artifacts, 99–103
    career portfolio, 31–32
    content and captions, 105–12
    job search portfolio, 62, 63
    prior–learning portfolio, 85
Computer technology. *See also* Electronic
    portfolio
    in distance learning, 85–86
    in occupational information systems, 56
Construction of portfolio, 136–39
Content and captions, 105–12. *See also*
    Components of portfolio
    adding quantifiable or numerical data,
      111–12
    analyzing audience, 108–9, 141
    creating captions and supporting text,
      109–11
    exercises, 108–9, 110–11
    number of samples to include, 107–8
    thinking like your customer, 106–7
Continuing education. *See* Lifelong learning
    portfolio
Cooks, *DOT* rating, 52
Corrigan, Dan, 85
Craft, Sonya S., 87
Creating portfolios, 5
    career portfolio, 35–57
    content and captions, 105–12
    crafting artifacts, 99–103
    design, 125–39
    first steps, 15
    organization, 113–23
Web pages, 149, 150–53, 156–59, 161
Creating Portfolios for Success in School,
    Work, and Life, 179
Cross–functional skills, identifying, 39–42

Customers, marketing to, 71

D

DA 2A/2B, 90
Damn Good Résumé, 180
Databases
    lifework, for career portfolio, 38–39, 43, 46,
      48
O*NET, 56
Data quantification, 111–12
Data skills, 170
    vocabulary for, 173–74
DD214, 90
Defense Language Proficiency Test, 90
Design of portfolio, 125–39
    books on, 180
    closing reflection, 135–36
    construction, 136
    front matter, 130–32
    highlights summary, 132, 134–35
    introductions, 133, 134, 137
    language checklist, 137–38
    on–line communications, 152–54, 156–57
    paper and sheet protectors, 138–39
    placement of materials, 126–27, 128
    simplicity, 128–30
    summary statements for sections, 136–37
    typography, 127–28, 129
The Dictionary of Holland Occupational
    Codes, 55, 182
Dictionary of Occupational Titles, 51–55
Direct mailing approaches, 61–62
Display table, 24–25
Distance learning, 79–80, 84–86
Dixon, Pam, 84
Documents
    archiving for personal portfolio, 26–29
    goal–setting, 169
    of lifework, 17–20
    military, 89–90
    prior learning for credit, 82–84
Does Your Résumé Wear Combat Boots?, 181
Donlan, Leni, 148
DOT, 51–55
DPT codes, 51–54
Drier, Harry, 95, 181
Dunham, Gail, 86
Duties, in lifework database, 38, 43, 46, 48

E

Editing by Design, 180
Education, 169. *See also* Lifelong learning
    portfolio
Educators, job search by, 34

Educator's Job Search, 181
EGOE, 55, 182
Electronic portfolio, 147–63
   design for on–line communications, 152–53
   e–mail and text–based communications,
     154–55
   future of, 149–52
   high–tech and low–tech strategies, 151
   keyword résumés, 155
   networking on Internet, 160–63
Web pages, 149, 150–53, 156–59, 161
Electronic Résumé Revolution, 182
Electronic University Network, 86
E–mail, 152, 154–55, 159, 161
Employee evaluations, 73–78
Employers
   value of military experience to, 88
   value of portfolios to, 13
Employment. *See also* Career advancement
     portfolio; Career portfolio; Job search
     portfolio
   temporary/mobile nature of, 9, 32–33
The End of Work, 33, 180
The Enhanced Guide for Occupational
     Exploration, 55, 182
Ethics, 106
Evaluation of employees
   portfolios and employee evaluation
     procedures, 75–78
   preparing for, 73–74
Evaluation of portfolio, final review, 141–45
Exercises
   analyzing audience, 108–9
   career portfolio
     analyzing artifacts using occupational
       codes, 53–54
     connecting artifacts to skills and
       outcomes, 44
     lifework database, 38–39
     looking at work thematically, 47–48
     skills identification, 39–42
     using ideal job to conceptualize new
       possibilities, 49
   personal portfolio, 21–22
   artifacts, 22–26
   warm–up, 21–22
   scoring rubric for portfolio, 142, 143
   warm–up, 15–16
   writing captions, 110–11

F

Feedback on portfolio, 57
Final review of portfolio, 141–45
   language and goals check, 142, 144–45

   scoring rubric, 142, 143, 145
Fitzpatrick, William G., 181
Front matter, 130–32
Functional organization, 113, 115–17
Future of virtual portfolios, 149–52
Future of work, 32–33, 147–49

G

Get Hired!, 181
Gill, Ann M., 179
Goals, career, 144
Goal–setting documents, 169
GOE, 54–55, 182
Good, C. Edward, 181
Grants, securing, 70
Graves, Donald H., 180
Green, Paul C., 181
Guerilla Tactics in the New Job Market, 181
The Guide for Occupational Exploration,
     54–55, 182

H

Handy, Charles, 32, 180
Harberger, Carol, 14
Help Wanted, An Inexperienced Job Seeker's
     Complete Guide to Career Success, 179
Highlights summary, 132, 134–35
Hiring process, job search portfolio and, 59–60
Holland, John, 55
Hook Up, Get Hired, 182
How NOT To Make It...And Succeed, 181
How to Make $1000 a Minute Negotiating Your
     Salaries and Raises, 117, 181
How to Prepare Your Portfolio, 62, 179
HTML codes, 153, 156
Humor, in portfolio creation, 28
Hypertext links, 152–53

I

Ideal jobs, 49–50
Imagine Loving Your Work, 47, 181
Informational interviews, portfolios taken to,
     55, 57
Information systems, occupational, digital
     frontier in, 56
Intellectual traits, vocabulary for, 177–78
Internet, 154
   e–mail, 152, 154–55, 159, 161
   job searching on, 153, 159
   networking on, 160–63
   security, 156
Web pages, 149, 150–53, 156–59, 161
The Internet University, 85, 182
Interview portfolio, 62–67

Interviews, informational, portfolios taken to, 55, 57
Introductions in portfolio, 133, 134, 137

J

Jackson, Tom, 181
Job codes *(DOT),* 51–54
Job experience, limited, 100
Job Interviewing for Dummies, 182
Job loss trauma, coping with, 42
Job performance evaluations, 73–78
Job Search Networking, 181
Job search portfolio, 59–71
  hiring process stages and, 59–60
  interview portfolio, 62–67
  marketing portfolio, 69–71
  networking and direct mailing approaches, 61–62
  portfolio–résumé hybrids, 60–61
  presentation, 65–69
  types, 64
Job search resources, 180–82
Job Shift, 32, 180

K

Kennedy, Joyce Lain, 150, 155
Key words, in résumé scanning, 60, 155
Kimeldorf, Martin, 179, 181

L

Language. *See also* Communication; Vocabulary
  for portfolio, 137–38, 144
  writing captions, exercise, 110–11
Lateral changes, 74–75
Learning. *See* Lifelong learning portfolio
Leng, Judith, 82
Lewis, Stephen M., 179
Licensing, portfolios used for, 81
Lifelong learning portfolio, 79–86
  assets managed with, 80–82
  case study, 82
  college career placement centers and, 86
  contents, 85
  continuous improvement, 79–80
  distance learning, 84–86
  documenting prior learning for credit, 82–84
  school related to work, 80
Lifework database, for career portfolio, 38–39, 43, 46, 48
Lifework documents, 17–20
Life Work Portfolio, 179
Loans, 70, 123

Looking Good in Print, 180

M

Maintaining portfolio, 73
Make Your Case, 5, 75
Manuelian, Peter Omar, 179
Marketing portfolio, 69–71
Marketing Yourself for a Second Career, 181
Marquand, Ed, 62, 179
Memory book, 21
Michigan State University, 86
Military skills and accomplishments, 87–95
  connecting military jobs to civilian positions, 88–89
  fictional stories, 93–95
  linking artifact to occupation, 93
  suggestions, 171
  transition training, 95
  translated to civilian employment needs, 91–93
  using existing military documents, 89–90
  value to employers, 87–88
  writing tips, 93
Miller–Tiedeman, Anna, 181
Mind–set for porfolios, 17–29
Morris, Gary, 156
Muzila, Patrik and Peter, 150–52

N

Networking, 61–62
  on Internet, 160–63
Numerical data, 111–12
Nurses, skills of, 36–37

O

Occupational Code Numbers, 51–54
Occupational information systems, digital frontier in, 56
Occupational Outlook Handbook, 182
Occupational resources, 51–55, 182
O*NET, 56
On–line communications. *See* Electronic portfolio
OOH, 182
Opton, David, 60
Organization of portfolio
  adapting résumé writing strategies, 114–15
  chronological, 113, 115, 116
  functional, 113, 115–17
  grouping data, 113–14
  outlining process, 122–23
  special report, 117, 120–21
  teaching–portfolio model, 121–22
  thematic, 117, 118–19

Web pages, 158–59
Outcomes
    in career portfolio, 41–42
    connecting artifacts to, 44
    job performance evaluations, 73–78
    in lifework database, 43, 46, 48
Outlining process, 122–23
Out of Uniform, 95, 181

P

Paper protectors, 138–39
Parker, Roger C., 180
Parker, Yana, 155, 180
Party game exercise, 23–26
People skills, 170–71
    vocabulary for, 174–75, 177–78
Performance reviews, 73–78
Personality words, 177–78
Personal portfolio, 17–29
    archiving for, 26–29
    artifacts for, 22–26
    beginning, 20–22
    lifework documents in, 17–20
    professional portfolio vs., 14
    suggestions, 167
Personal touch, in job search portfolio, 63
Peterson, Neil, 32
Peterson's Guide to Distance Learning, 85, 182
The PLA Guide to Internet Job Searching, 153, 182
Portfolio Development Handbook, Prior Learning Experience Program, 179
Portfolio Development Independent Study Guide 7, 179
Portfolio Portraits, 180
Portfolio–résumé hybrids, 60–61
Portfolios. *See also* Components of portfolios; Creating portfolios; Exercises
    artifacts, 99–103
    author's credentials, 1–2
    career, 31–57
    career advancement, 73–78
    content and captions, 105–12
    current interest in, vii, 3–4
    definition, 12
    design, 125–39
    electronic, 147–63
    employer–friendly, 13
    ethical, 106
    example, 14–15
    final review, 141–45
    hiring experience, 2–3
    job search, 59–71
    lifelong learning, 79–86

    military skills and accomplishments, 87–95
    mind–set for, 17–29
    number of samples in (size of), 107–8
    organization, 113–23
    personal, 17–29
    power of, 11–16, 31
    with prescribed criteria or outlines, 123
    professional vs. personal, 14
    stories, 4–5
    suggestions for, 167, 169–71
Presentation of portfolio at interview, 65–69
Princeton Review Gopher site, 86
Prior–learning portfolio model, 83–84
Professional portfolio, 11–16. *See also* Portfolios
Promotions, preparing for, 73–74
Psychologists, *DOT* rating, 52
Publications on portfolios, 179–80

Q

Quantifiable data, 111–12

R

Rakes, Thom, 80
Reports, special, 117, 120–21
Resources, 179–82
Responsibilities, in lifework database, 38, 43, 46, 48
Responsibility indicators, vocabulary for, 177
Résumé–portfolio hybrids, 60–61
Résumés, 59–60
    adapting writing strategies for portfolio, 114–15
    organization, 113–14
    scanning, 60, 155
Rifkin, Jeremy, 33, 180
Riley, Margaret F., 102, 153, 157, 161

S

Sanborn, Jane, 4
Schlueter, Ken, 87, 89
Seasonal artifacts, 22–23
Seattle Times, 32
Selden, Peter, 121, 180
Self, expanded view of, 42
Self–absorption, in portfolio creation, 28
Self-Directed Search, 55, 182
Shapiro, Phil, 151
Sheet protectors, 138–39
Sherbert, Sue, 107
Simplicity in design, 128–30
Skill–factoring, 36, 39–40
Skills
    in career portfolio, 33–34

conceived in broad terms, 36–38
identifying, 39–42
connecting artifacts to, 44
interview, 64
in lifework database, 43, 46, 48
military, 87–95
in professional portfolio, 11–16
valuable, 47
vocabulary for, 173–75
work samples illustrating, 170–71
Smith, Catherine, 4, 5, 75
Special reports, 117, 120–21
Starting portfolio
career portfolio, 31–32
personal portfolio, 20–26
Start–up loans, 70
Stevens, Paul, 74, 180
Summary statements for portfolio sections,
136–37
Sunstein, Bonnie S., 180

T

Teachers, job search by, 34
The Teaching Portfolio, 121, 180
Teaching–portfolio model, 121–22
Teamwork, vocabulary for, 177
Text, supporting, creating, 109–12
Thayer, Vicki, 181
Thematic organization, 117, 118–19
Thornton, Marty, 3
Tour of Duty Chronicle, 180
Training, 169
Transferable skills, identifying, 39–42
Typography, 127–28, 129

U

University of Northern Iowa, 81

V

Value of portfolios, 11–16, 31
Verification of Military Education (VMET),
89–90
VGM's Guide to Temporary Employment, 181
Vick, Bill, 148
Virtual College, 84–85, 182
Virtual portfolio. *See* Electronic portfolio
Visual appeal. *See* Design of portfolio
VMET, 89–90
Vocabulary
for military skills and accomplishments, 93
personality words, 177–78
in résumé scanning, 60, 155
for skills, 173–75

W

Web pages. *See* World Wide Web pages
What Color Is Your Parachute?, 55, 181
White, Jan V., 180
Words. *See* Key words; Vocabulary
Work
future of, 32–33, 147–49
school related to, 80
viewed thematically, 47–48
Work habits, vocabulary for, 177
Work performance, 169–70
Work samples, 107–8, 170–71
World Wide Web pages, 149, 153, 156, 161
case study, 150–52
design, 152–53, 156–57
organizing, 158–59
storing portfolio items, 158
Writing captions, 110–11

Conduct a Winning Job Search with These New Peterson's Titles

The 90-Minute Interview Prep Book
Peggy Schmidt
Shows you how to make preparing for job interviews *easy and effective* by working with a "coach"—friend, spouse, colleague, or even yourself. *Free software* provides checklists and evaluation forms for critiquing your presentation style.
ISBN 634-0, 160 pp., 8 1/2 x 11, $15.95 pb

The Job Hunter's Word Finder
James Bluemond
Give your resume or cover letter the needed extra "punch" with an A-Z guide to thousands of synonyms for overused words, the latest industry-specific buzzwords for 100 career fields, and key words for each job position.
ISBN 600-6, 224 pp., 6 x 9, $12.95 pb

Personal Job Power
Clay Carr and Valorie Beer
Helps you survive—and thrive—in today's uncertain business world. Shows you how to develop and use personal power effectively. Identifies seven different "power types" and shows how each one works.
ISBN 599-9, 224 pp., 6 x 9, $12.95 pb

Hidden Job Market 1997
Provides you with detailed contact information on the nation's 2,000 fastest-growing small to mid-size companies—those that are *hiring at four times* the national rate! Covers a wide range of high-growth industries such as environmental consulting, genetic engineering, and computers.
ISBN 644-8, 320 pp., 6 x 9, $18.95 pb

Job Opportunities in Business 1997
Describes 2,000 of the leading fastest-growing U.S. companies in the service and trade sectors as well as manufacturing and industrial firms.
ISBN 646-4, 334 pp., 8 1/2 x 11, $21.95 pb

Job Opportunities in Engineering & Technology 1997
Profiles some 2,000 companies at the leading edge of high-technology in areas such as biotechnology, telecommunications, software, computers and peripherals, and consumer electronics.
ISBN 647-2, 432 pp., 8 1/2 x 11, $21.95 pb

Job Opportunities in Health Care 1997
Identifies hiring organizations in the health-care field, including medical equipment and supply companies, pharmaceutical firms, health insurance and managed-care companies, skilled nursing care facilities, hospitals, and medical laboratories.
ISBN 648-0, 220 pp., 8 1/2 x 11, $21.95 pb

ISBN Prefix: 1-56079-

Available at Fine Bookstores Near You

Or Order Direct
Call: 800-338-3282
Fax: 609-243-9150

Visit Peterson's Education & Career Center
on the Internet
http://www.petersons.com

P Peterson's Princeton, NJ